A PRACTICAL GUIDE TO EFFECTIVE PRESENTATION

It's Not Just What You Say,

It's How You Say It That Gets Results

A PRACTICAL GUIDE

TO EFFECTIVE PRESENTATION

*It's Not Just What You Say,
It's How You Say It That Gets Results*

Rex P. Gatto, Ph.D.

GTA Press

Pittsburgh ◆ 1990

Copyright © 1990 by Dr. Rex P. Gatto. All rights reserved. No part of this book may be reproduced or utilized in any form or by any means without written permission of the copyright holder.

Library of Congress Cataloging-In-Publication Data.

Gatto, Rex P.

A Practical Guide to Effective Presentation: It's Not Just What You Say, It's How You Say It That Gets Results.

Catalog Number: 90-083272

ISBN 0-945997-20-5

published by

GTA Press

733 Washington Road, Suite 107

Pittsburgh, PA 15228

Printed in the United States of America

I have dreamed

and made it a reality

because of Mickey, Shawn, and Maura.

TABLE OF CONTENTS

CHAPTER 1
The Myth of Presentation.. 1

CHAPTER 2
Effective Presentation and the Role of the Presenter............7

CHAPTER 3
The Initial Presentation Design.. 21

CHAPTER 4
Presentment: The Big Picture.. 43

CHAPTER 5
Presentment: The Essential Elements................................71

CHAPTER 6
Presenting In A Business Meeting................................... 133

CHAPTER 7
Feedback.. 159

IN CLOSING
....169

REFERENCES
....173

PREFACE

We all give daily presentations: formally or informally we speak to colleagues and clients, in person and over the phone. All of these presentations share a common loose structure. You present, someone listens (or receives), and an information exchange takes place. The concept of exchanging information is the most complex function in the workplace today.

This book offers alternative approaches to presentation that will help you focus on what you want to accomplish and to do so effectively.

Many people have written about presentation as though it were a stigma to business. Great satirical techniques such as, "don't look at the audience," "picture your audience naked wearing only red socks," or "consider your audience as people of lesser intelligence," are used by speakers to build self-confidence. Yet these techniques address only the most basic fear speakers experience, that of being in the limelight.

You'll join a group of colleagues and unabashedly present, yet when asked to stand, your heart palpitates, your mouth becomes dry, your hands sweat, and your mind quickly flips through information. A successful presenter makes use of a participating audience rather than speaking to an isolated group of "red socks." By being prepared, you can relax, use your presentation design, and your ability to lessen nervousness—your own as well as the audience's. This book will help you build upon your presentation abilities and skills. You will develop confidence in yourself because you'll understand and use the art of presentation.

There is no secret to good presentations, but there are a number of techniques that, when coupled with hard work, can make a presentation seem magical. The content must be shaped in a way that allows the presenter to come across as sincere. The difference between attending a presentation and reading an essay is the human dynamic. The exchange of content—what the presenter offers, how the presenter says it, and the emotional interplay between the presenter and the audience—can change a dry reading into a stimulating presentation.

This book offers various methodologies for presentation; it suggests ways to organize and shape content so that the presenter's style gives body to the presentation. Finally, this book asks questions that can invigorate presenters with enthusiasm and creativity.

In working through this book, you will discover and develop your style of presentation. Then, through practice and feedback, you will become an effective presenter; opening and expanding your talents as a communicator.

A PRACTICAL GUIDE TO EFFECTIVE PRESENTATION

It's Not Just What You Say,

It's How You Say It That Gets Results

CHAPTER 1

THE MYTH OF PRESENTATION

> *"Communication is basic to group development which would suggest that the more open and unrestricted the communication the better."*
>
> *(Luft, 1984, p. 125)*

This book is meant to be a thought-provoking resource, rather than a blueprint to effective presentation. It provides suggestions that are available when presenting, based on what the presenter wants to accomplish. It provides answers to two of the most important questions presenters must face: "Why should the audience listen to me?" and "How can results of the presentation be measured?"

Because we discuss issues daily while on the phone, in hallways, and at meetings, formally or informally, we make presentations. What are the differences between formal and informal presentations?

A formal presentation should have a prescribed outcome, a strategy or planning design that describes when, what, and how to present, and it must have a way to measure the audience's response to the presentation (which is called follow-up).

Often in today's business arena, executives, managers, and professionals think that because they know something, they can present it effectively. Yet effective presenting requires more than exchanging ideas (although exchanging ideas is a part of presentation). Often professionals state that they do not have time to plan their presentations; but, given the power of a good presentation, do they have time not to prepare?

Remember: a presentation goes far beyond the content; the human dynamic that "sells" the content makes a difference. If the dynamic is focused and geared toward the listener's mental and physical involvement, the presentation will be successful.

Have you ever noticed that one person can present, with little audience reaction, while another person presents to the same group and the audience comes alive? Presentation is the art of one-on-one interaction, of presenter to listener. An effective orator can simultaneously evoke emotion and stimulate our intellects and curiosity. The difference among presenters is how they practice and plan to achieve what they want to achieve. It is important to practice and experiment as a presenter to establish what you are capable of doing and what you want to accomplish.

For all speakers, nervousness is a major aspect of a presentation. People continually state that the fear, or anxiety, of presenting is always with them. As early as 1926, Dale Carnegie wrote:

Many have written statements telling why they enrolled for this training and what they hoped to obtain from it. Naturally, the phraseology varied, but the central desire in these letters, the basic want in the vast majority, remained surprisingly the same: 'When I am called upon to stand up and speak,' man after man wrote, 'I become so self-conscious, so frightened, I can't think clearly, can't concentrate, can't remember what I intended to say. I want to gain self-confidence, poise, and the ability to think on my feet. I want to get my thoughts together in logical order and I want to be able to say my say clearly and convincingly before a business group or audience.' (p. 9)

Not much has changed since Dale Carnegie made this observation. Managers today have two great anxiety provokers due to their work: conducting performance appraisals and making presentations. For presentations, we will design a pragmatic approach to improve, which also will help in other aspects of your job as a communicator.

There is a phenomenon that occurs in presentation: As knowledgeable presenters we can speak comfortably for hours, but when called upon to stand and say a few words to a group, we are enveloped with fear. What happens? There's no real answer to this question. We must trust ourselves to present facts and ideas acceptably and develop a support system for ourselves. How can we accomplish this? Practicing, knowing how to shape a presentation, using your strengths as a presenter, and knowing different styles of speaking, thinking, and listening are all ways to conquer fear. Fear of presentation is fear of an unknown outcome. Have confidence: no one in the audience knows what you will say next, but if you have organized and planned your presentation, you know the outcome. Trust yourself to know the what (the content) and how (presentation style) well enough to clearly and logically present and persuade your listeners. The key is self-confidence, which comes with knowing that you can successfully and effectively present. Your support mechanism is your presentation outline and visual aids.

Confidence in presenting comes from an understanding of your abilities—from knowing what you do well in a presentation—and using those skills to develop a relationship with the listener. Keep in mind that a presentation is a one-to-one relationship. Each person interprets what you say and comprehends it in his or her individual manner. By focusing, planning your design, knowing the expected outcome, and by understanding your skills and the needs of your audience, you can become a successful and effective presenter.

DEFINITIONS

Next we will define some ideas central to designing an effective presentation.

Effective Presentation

Effective presentation involves establishing a mutual understanding of information between the speaker and the audience, given the speaker's abilities and skills and the audience's ability to comprehend within today's business environment. Most often this process involves visual and verbal communication. An effective presentation defines what the presenter wants to accomplish, why the audience should listen or what they might gain, and what results or outcomes are possible.

Responsibility for Presenting

Responsibility involves accepting your role as a presenter and using your ability, the environment, and the available resources to address the audience's needs. Are you willing to give the time needed to prepare, to collect information about the topic and audience, to focus and shape the presentation, to share your humanness with your audience, and to have fun during the process?

Quality Presentation

A quality presentation makes use of the presenter's skills and abilities (including facial expression and nonverbal gestures) and the appropriate media sources (slides, flip charts, films, videos, overhead transparencies, etc.); the appropriate content (considering the knowledge level of the audience); supplemental material (notebooks, manuals, references, handouts); and the appropriate style or mode of presenting (to the point, question-and-answers, problem solving, humorous, very structured, etc.).

Presentation Skill

Presentation skill is the application of your knowledge and ability over changing periods of time when you are relaxed or stressed. Furthermore, it is the interactive adaptation of your ability to communicate in an environment with particular people and/or equipment. Your presentation skill is the exposure or level of your abilities which the audience perceives.

The act of communicating creates some stress, even if only two people are involved. This stress level increases when one person must address several others. Most people find giving a presentation an anxious experience; they fear not performing well. Planning for this sort of anxiety—or planning to succeed in spite of it—will lessen your fears. Think of ways to build a support system for yourself. You might organize your presentation on note cards, or design different support media (such as slides or charts). Plan to use your presentation skill—your techniques for shaping your content and involving your audience—rather than your presentation ability—your knowledge of the subject itself.

CHAPTER 2

EFFECTIVE PRESENTATION AND THE ROLE OF THE PRESENTER

> "To live the life of self-expression requires courage. To love greatly, to admit one's hate without having it destroy one's equilibrium, to express anger when it is genuine, to rise to heights of joy and know deep sorrow, to go on for adventures in spite of loneliness, to catch lofty ideas and carry them into action—in short, to live out infinite number of instinctual urges that rise in glorious challenge within one requires courage.
>
> *(May, 1989, p. 156)*

Whatever the goals of your presentation, they are accomplished more efficiently when others understand your intentions and form their understanding through your presentation of ideas. A speaker develops effective presentation skills by establishing efficient, systematic, and unique strategies for presenting ideas through visual, verbal, and nonverbal communication. Your appearance, enthusiasm, voice inflection, eye contact, and manner of presenting the message bring meaning to what you say. It's not just what you say, but how you say it that persuades your audience. Your presentation becomes the message.

A speaker should be "other-directed," or focused on the audience's needs, rather than "self-directed," or focused on your own perception of the material. Probably the greatest flaw in corporate presentations is that the presenter bases the presentation on personal terminology, background, and emotional excitement without considering the audience. An other-directed presenter asks, "What's in it for the audience? Why should they listen to me?" The answer to these questions will be specific to each audience. People have unique mannerisms and different ways of conceptualizing information, and a presenter must anticipate and acknowledge the idiosyncrasies and unique perceptions of each audience.

Effective presentation skills are based on your ability to recognize and address individual characteristics and to "tailor" your personality to the needs of the audience. When you make a presentation, you give it on two levels: (1) content is disseminated, shared, or collected; and (2) the audience responds emotionally to what is said and how it is said.

Effective presentation exists when the majority of the audience clearly understands the information presented and is responsive to the expectations or goals of the presenter. In terms of these two factors, a

Effective Presentation and the Role of the Presenter 9

presentation message, or at least the effect of the message, is measurable. For instance, imagine that a speaker offers a presentation introducing a new policy or action for the company. After the presentation, if the action or policy is not implemented successfully, it's possible that the audience did not comprehend the use or application of the expected related actions or results.

The only way to measure results is to know what results are expected. A speaker must ask: "What results do I want? What expectations do I have in presenting this content? What expectations might the audience have?" No presenter is all things to all people; however, you must realize that a presentation is not just sharing something about which you are knowledgeable. You must consider how your knowledge is presented and shaped. Effective presentation establishes with the audience the understanding necessary for a transfer of information that is harmonious and focused on achieving corporate, departmental, office, supervisory, educational, and individual expectations.

Think of a presentation as a steak dinner. To enjoy the steak you must cut one piece, chew, swallow, and begin to digest. Similarly, an audience ideally is presented with small amounts of information, or parts of an idea, which they listen to, contemplate, and digest.

Just as you shouldn't fill your mouth with five pieces of steak, a presenter shouldn't offer too many ideas or facts at once. The brain needs time to assimilate, compare, and identify ways to understand and apply information. Too much data presented in too short a time might result in "mental indigestion" for the audience. A presenter only creates confusion by presenting too many facts without letting the listener contemplate and digest that information. Because a listener can only take in so much—and a presenter can only offer so much—in a given time frame, you also must limit material to the time available.

In addition, an effective presenter supports this process of mental digestion by taking time to explain information, and by guiding listeners to an understanding of how they might individually apply what they learn. This explaining and guiding gives shape and structure to the information a presenter must offer.

Imagine a potential presentation as an artist's blank canvas, as a potential painting. The artist might use colors or black and white, abstract, realism, or a mixture of many styles. A presenter has the same options. A presenter begins with silence, but is capable of verbally "painting" with colorful terms, or black-and-white oppositions, using abstract or concrete ideas, much as an artist paints on canvas.

In guiding the audience's understanding, a presenter should shape information in a way that is mutually understood by the presenter and listener; you must share the same language and the same level of comprehension with the audience so that both have a basis for discussion and, eventually, for application or implementation.

For this reason a presenter should begin with an overview, "paint a big picture" in general terms, and then guide the listener toward a more specific understanding and analysis of what is said. This is accomplished through several verbal and nonverbal techniques. For instance, a face-to-face presentation consists of a speaker (who acts as a moving visual) influencing the audience through eye contact, attire, facial expression, speech patterns, and so on. In an effective presentation, the rapport established between the presenter and the listener(s) is as important as the information the presenter wants to disseminate.

Rapport refers to a sympathetic and harmonious communication between the audience and the speaker. For the audience, it includes a certain amount of emotional buy-in, a feeling of "Okay, this makes sense," or "This is plausible or realistic," or "This person understands my needs." Again, anticipating and understanding the needs of your audience is crucial to a presentation; you must know what is to be accomplished, and must choose a presentation format that will help you to achieve your goals. In a presentation, two factors occur simultaneously: content must be shared, and the listener must respond mentally. How well you verbally paint a picture, and build a "comparative conduit" that helps the audience move between general and specific terms and perceptions of the subject, will directly affect your success in creating a mutual understanding among all those participating.

Effective presentation, then, is the collecting, disseminating, and sharing of information so that follow-up action occurs.

A presentation begins before you speak and continues after you leave. You must know why you are presenting and realize that, in terms of understanding and action, a presentation must continue well after you finish. Sometimes a presenter's greatest influence is felt after a presentation, when the listener reflects upon what was said. This reflection period is actually what separates an "okay" presentation from a powerful, thought-provoking presentation that influences follow-up and/or expected results. A presentation that is not provocative or memorable probably won't remain in the listener's mind and stimulate further thought.

Effective presentation is not just content; it must include the dynamic interaction that occurs between two people, even if there are hundreds of people in the audience. Essentially, a presentation works between two people: you (the presenter), with your style of communication, working, learning, and personality and physical movements; and the listener, who receives information with a unique style of learning, working, communicating, and interacting. Each person individually interprets the presenter's words and demonstration. This process occurs within a continual state of flux, because a presentation can be affected by the time of day it is given, by the speaker's and the audience's prior content knowledge, by the audience's biases toward different styles of presenting, by the stress the speaker and the audience feel, and by the environment.

Presentation is dependent upon the situation in which the presenter and listener find themselves. It is important to continually assess listeners, to ask: "Why are they here?" "What do I want to accomplish? What is in it for the listener?" We might ask ourselves why any listener should consider what the presenter says as worthwhile. Keep in mind there are two sides of presentation: (1) content; and (2) speaker dynamics (rapport, emotional "buy-in", etc.).

Many technical people fall into the trap of thinking, "I know the material, so I can present the content," but this assumption isn't necessarily true. Many knowledgeable speakers are also boring and long-winded. They choose no focus; in a one-hour presentation they attempt to explain everything they've ever learned or experienced. Unfortunately, we have all sat through these kinds of presentations. Life is too short to put yourself—and your audience—through this! As a presenter, know what you want and actively work to achieve it. A successful presentation is not a mystery; it is the collection, and sharing of information in an appropriate manner that takes into consideration the ability and skill of the presenter, the intelligence and interest of the listener, and the situation, so that the presenter and the listener benefit.

DEVELOPING AN AWARENESS OF EFFECTIVE PRESENTATION

In a presentation, information is usually delivered verbally. However, verbal skills alone might not effectively meet the audience's needs. Visual modes, such as diagrams, written messages, and so on, are often beneficial when disseminating information. As a presenter, it is essential that you use different communication modes, given your ability, available resources, and the presentation environment.

The listener(s) must perceive information before comprehending it, and the extent to which a listener understands information is affected by the way it is presented. Thus, it is important to know the different ways information is perceived, and to have some sense of how each relates to the individual's comprehension.

We all know there are five senses: sight, hearing, touch, smell, and taste. Sight (visual) and hearing (aural) are the two senses used most often to gather information. Most presentations depend most heavily on visual and aural aids. The sense of touch also can greatly influence an educational and working environment. On a personal level, we know a handshake can influence a first impression. A pen or pencil might not have the "right" feel. An uncomfortable chair might alter the awareness (and thus influence the perceptions) of a person sitting in it. A presenter should consider each of the senses as a potential line of communication to his audience.

For example, you might supplement a presentation with handouts or other visual aids printed on heavy, glossy paper that is pleasant to hold. Materials that appeal to or please the senses catch the listener's attention on an emotional level and encourage the person to be intellectually receptive to the presenter's information. A manager introducing new equipment to staff might pass around a model or introduce the equipment itself, if possible, while describing new operating procedures.

In addition, certain occupations, such as chef or chemist, require greater dependency on the senses of smell and taste. When you prepare for a particular group of people, you should consider these avenues as part of the preparation. For instance, if you prepare a presentation—say, to suggest that a group of chemists invest in a new company—you would certainly distribute a product sample. You might describe the product while they examine it, suggesting that they smell it, and so on.

Typically the senses of smell and taste are used the least in our educational and working environments. While the presentation noted previously might work well for chemists, its effect might be lost on a group of engineers. A presenter must consider what particular senses the audience might use and appropriate ways to appeal to those senses.

People have unique learning styles that influence their perception and comprehension. Many people, however, are not aware that their strongest perceptual need, in the area of communication, is visual. Most audiences recall best material that was visually presented or reinforced. Both the presenter, offering information, and the listener, receiving and understanding information, should be concerned with three aspects of communication: the collection, dissemination, and sharing of information.

Collecting Information

Reading or listening to acquire information.

Disseminating Information

Writing, explaining, or stating precise facts that are supported by valid research, outlining a procedure to be followed, and so on.

Sharing Information

The combined acts of writing and reading, or speaking and listening to, information in an effort to question or reinforce collected information. The sharing of information can stimulate many new ideas in a listener that alone the person might never have thought.

When presenting you must be aware of the recipient's information needs, as well as your own style of presenting. If you like or dislike someone, you might respond to that bias, rather than neutrally addressing that person's statement or question. The primary thought pattern of the brain is that of comparison; we ask ourselves, "Did I know this?" "Is it right?" "Do I agree?" "Let me analyze it." "How can I use it?" Each of these questions is based on comparison.

This is an important point. An audience compares a speaker to other presenters; what and how you present, your position, your dress, is measured against their expectations. A presenter should try to put forth a clear, unequivocal statement both verbally and visually. You should not let your appearance or demeanor work against your words, or vice versa. A speaker who presents the subject as though he/she would rather be doing something else will not be effective. You should be aware of your needs and the audience's needs. Your physical response to the time of day (are you a "morning person" or is your energy level higher at night?), your physical needs, as well as the comprehension level of the audience, the room temperature and setup, lighting, and every other concept you might imagine.

Effective Presentation and the Role of the Presenter

One statement will always be true: The audience will have an opinion about you and what you have to say. You have to shape the audience's opinion by being aware of what and why you are presenting. You set the climate or tone through your manner of presentation.

It is important to realize that you might have a dominant style of perceiving what influences the way you present information. How do you usually collect, disseminate, and share information? Do you send memos or discuss issues verbally? Does your style meet the needs of the audience? You can only answer "yes" to the last question if you utilize different modes of presentation to meet the audience's comprehension needs.

Again, the first function of the thinking process is to compare information. We constantly compare our traditions, values, general knowledge, standards, and expectations with the new information that continually bombards our minds. Collecting, disseminating, and sharing accurate information is imperative in our attempt to guide the mental comparison of old and new concepts. This sharing of information takes into consideration the presenter's motivations in giving information, and the listener's preferences in actively receiving that information. Together the speaker and listener create an unambiguous, mutual understanding of the presented information.

Both visual and verbal modes should be utilized to satisfy the audience's different perceptual preferences. Perception is the first step toward creating ideas.

The following steps provide an outline of the mental processes of perception and comprehension. An effective presenter can guide listeners through each step of the process.

Step 1 **Acquiring Information**

    A.   Taking in the information through the senses.

    B.   Concentrating on the information.

    C.   Focusing without rebuttal.

Step 2 **Comparing**

    A.   Did I know the information?

    B.   Is this new information?

    C.   Do I agree?

    D.   Do I disagree?

    E.   My experience is . . . .

Step 3 **Innovation**

    A.   Could this information be used this way?

    B.   Could this information be adapted to my old information?

    C.   This information could create a new . . . .

Step 4 Influences

- A. Methods of collecting, disseminating, and sharing information.
- B. Personality.
- C. Appearance (mannerisms and attire).
- D. Position of authority.
- E. Personal needs.
- F. Willingness to receive the information.

Step 5 Synergism

- A. A combination of the first four steps.
- B. Developing, applying, and evaluating concepts.
- C. Realizing that any combination of people is unique, and as a whole, the group has potential far beyond individual potential.

Step 6 Conclusion

- A. Utilize your dominant perception. You should use the most comfortable style to increase your awareness.
- B. Use every method (verbal and visual) available to you (video, documents, small group discussions, explanation, etc.).

Summary

Clearly there is more to a presentation than "knowing" your material. There are two sides to presenting: content and perception (emotional buy-in). An effective presenter must create a collaborative relationship with the listener. It is also the presenter's job to promote an environment in which the listener wants to listen, take in, and apply information in an appropriate manner.

Effective presentation is not a mystery. It is a combination of selecting the appropriate information; developing strategy to arrange it; designing the format; presenting; reassessing the presentation; and, if possible, following up or determining application after the presentation.

CHAPTER 3

THE INITIAL PRESENTATION DESIGN

"The words and sentences of which language is composed are said to be tools used to express meanings, thoughts, ideas, propositions, emotions, needs, desires, and many other things in and on the speaker's mind.

(Skinner, 1976, p. 98)

USING AN OUTLINE

Designing a presentation helps the speaker format and shape ideas and style. Before you can design a presentation, you must ask yourself several questions.

Why Am I Speaking?

An effective presenter must identify the results expected from a presentation. The entire focus of the presentation should be geared to address the questions, "Why am I speaking?" and "What do I, as the presenter, want to accomplish?" The latter question is crucial to a presentation; it can mean the difference between a logical, well-designed presentation and an "I know this stuff, I'll wing it" discussion. You should have a focused direction for your goals, the presentation content, and the audience. It is your responsibility to determine the "why's" of your presentation, and you must establish a viewpoint designed to address these issues.

What's In It for the Audience?

To begin an outline, it's a good idea to address each of these three questions: "Why am I speaking?" "What do I want to accomplish?" and "Why should the audience listen?" List each question on a separate sheet of paper. Then answer each question as completely and thoroughly as possible (list even minor thoughts). If time permits, put these papers away for a few hours or days, then read them again. Now, write one or two clear sentences that specifically state, "Why am I speaking?" "What do I want to accomplish?" and "Why should the audience listen?" Then reflect on the concepts for shaping and presenting material (Chapter 1). Finally, list all of the supportive materials you'll need to effectively present your topic and shape your presentation.

With Whom Am I Speaking?

Write what you think is the comprehension level of your audience and their basic needs. Sometimes this description will be general (e.g., "I don't know; mixed experiences"). Determine if it is a sophisticated audience (very knowledgeable, aware of the latest information, and educated in this content area) or a naive audience (this topic is basically new information for them). If you face a mixed audience, use that to your advantage; acknowledge that the audience is mixed in your opening, and offer both general and specific questions. If you feel comfortable breaking the audience into small groups, do so. Ask the groups to pool their general and specific information and discuss it. You might also ask the small groups to generate questions they'd like addressed. Consider your time limits. Don't allow the groups to overdo it. In an hour-long presentation, 10-15 minutes should be sufficient.

Concerning a predominantly naive audience, a rule of thumb is to present in general terms, to focus on benefits, and to avoid becoming specific too soon. On the other hand, with a sophisticated audience, providing a brief overview before delving into the specifics will suffice. A naive audience cannot analytically process new information as quickly, or on the same level, as people with a great deal of knowledge in that content area might. The presenter must shape a presentation so that it meets the audience's needs and creates a mutual understanding with the audience, as well as creating a level of discourse among the members of the audience.

Consider this analogy: A parent asks a pediatrician a question about his sick child, and he receives a response full of medical jargon. Most parents would fall into the category of a naive audience, and the physician is a sophisticated presenter. This is a classic example of a presentation that does not create a mutual understanding. The audience (parent) does not understand the technical medical presentation, and he will feel helpless and perhaps frustrated because his needs haven't yet been met. When presenting, the education level of the audience is very important.

Question: What should you do when you don't know the competence level of your audience? How might you go about accomplishing your goals?

Present an overview, share your own experiences, ask for questions or offer questions other audiences generally ask. This strategy "seeds" the audience with questions. Ask yourself questions, then ask the audience, "Has this happened to you?" or "Have you asked yourself . . .?" Wait for a reaction from the audience, such as nodding heads, then answer the question. Next, ask members of the audience to share their own experiences. Call on people who nodded their heads or showed interest earlier. As a presenter, you can set any reasonable ground rules: You decide when to ask questions, hand out information, schedule breaks, and so on. Use this to your advantage with an unknown audience; if you identify and address the right questions to the audience, you will learn how to present to them effectively.

The Initial Presentation Design

However, the reverse—identifying and addressing only the right answers—is not true. Having answers might not produce an effective presentation. Too often we have all been academically nurtured to "know," or at least to offer, answers. Similarly, through business experiences we often draw conclusions, but what is the question? We often don't ask. Knowing answers and presenting conclusions usually produces plenty of content, but this information might not address the right questions.

How Long Should I Speak?

This depends on what you want to accomplish. If you are told to speak for one hour, prepare and practice for a forty-five minute presentation. Generally give yourself fifteen to twenty minutes less than the allotted time. Presenters react to their audiences, and the audience to their presenter. A speaker might pick up on the audience's facial expressions and think, "I need to repeat this concept." An audience might respond by asking more specific questions, or by sharing their own experiences with the group. All of these enhance the presentation, so allow extra time for them. Don't cram an hour presentation into an hour. Relax your time frame.

This rule also allows for situations when you are forced to shorten your planned presentation. For instance, if you are the last speaker of three, and you're asked to cut your presentation, relax; don't cram a presentation planned for an hour into twenty minutes. Give your overview, if possible, ask for questions, and then offer a quick summary. Be flexible. Also, speakers tend to vary the speed of a verbal presentation. Allow time to emphasize a point, pause, repeat, or slowly state a thought. No matter how you practice your presentation, flow time will change with the audience present. Presenters can speak as fast as a couple of words a second (about 120 words per minute) or as slow as two or three words every five seconds. These average "speech speeds" can be effective and both greatly affect the time of a presentation.

Our three primary questions—Why? With whom? and How long?—should be set up in an outline format and addressed each time you plan a presentation. This outline, because it begins with your goals and the needs of your audience, will guide you toward shaping an effective presentation.

TYPES OF PRESENTATION

Do you intend your presentation to be persuasive or informative? Ask yourself, "Am I encouraging the audience to adopt my ideas, or am I informing them on this subject, or both?" As a presenter, you must be aware of the role you assume for each particular presentation. What is your motive in presenting this information? You must be clear on this question before you can make it clear to the audience.

Does your presentation have to agree with, precede, or follow another presentation? If you are giving a presentation in conjunction with another presentation, if your presentation complements a preceding presentation (even one that occurred a week earlier), then you must build a bridge between the two; you must explain and develop the connections between them for your audience.

Outline of Presentation Design Questions

1. Why am I speaking?
2. What do I want to accomplish by giving the presentation?
3. Why should the audience listen to me?
4. With whom am I speaking?
5. How long should I speak?
6. Is this presentation to be persuasive or informative?
7. Does this presentation have to agree with, precede, or follow another presentation?
8. How should the material be presented?

As you review these outline questions, note that they create a structure that will shape and support a presentation. Use this question outline to build your own presentation design.

SECTIONS OF A PRESENTATION

There are three sections in a presentation: (a) overview, (b) body, and (c) summary. As you design a presentation you must relate the outline questions to your content, developing the three sections of your presentation.

Overview

An overview introduces you and your subject matter, and it sets the parameters for your presentation.

- Introduction/Greeting
- Presenter and topic
- Objectives (measurable outcomes)
- A clear statement in the objectives that provokes thought, that acts as a "grabber" for the audience
- Ground rules (length of presentation, questions and answers, breaks, etc.)
- Specific topics
- Benefits: "What will the audience gain by listening?"

As an example, consider this overview:

Good morning, my name is Dr. Rex Gatto (greeting and introduction) and I am going to discuss, 'What Makes an Effective Presentation' (topic). There is no one right way to present (grabber). Each presentation depends on the speaker's ability to present, the audience's abilities to comprehend, and the situation—the time of day, stress, needs, desire, etc.

Over the next two hours I will present how to prepare and design a presentation. Today we will discuss these two points concerning effective presentation (ground rules).

There is no scheduled break, so if you feel like standing or moving about, please do so. I would like you to ask questions at the end of the presentation; however, please write your questions down as you contemplate them (ground rules supported by visuals). The first concept we will discuss is preparation, how to prepare by asking the right questions, and second, how to design and develop a presentation (specifics). This will help you design and present your information (benefit).

Again, this is only a sample of what a presenter might say and do; you might change it, depending on what you want to accomplish and the sophistication of your audience. After the overview, the presenter moves to the body of the presentation by giving the audience specific information.

Body

The body of the presentation includes specific information; details that support the topics stated in the overview. To continue with our example:

When you begin to prepare a presentation, you must ask yourself the right questions: "Why am I speaking?" An effective presenter must know what is to be accomplished through the presentation.

The length and depth of specific or detailed presentations depend on the same three criteria:

- Why are you speaking, and what do you want to accomplish?
- What are the abilities of the presenter and listeners? (For instance, what is their academic or work experience?)
- What is appropriate information, given the circumstances?

To bring all of the information together, it is important to build a bridge between the specific information and the overview. For example: Preparation is the first step in developing an effective presentation. It is important to continually remind the audience of the purpose and the application of the specifics or details you offer. A good presenter does this often enough to create continuity for his audience.

Unfortunately, many technical presentations highlight specific and/or detailed information without indicating why it's important or relating it to the "big picture." You should use visuals to support your message, and your message should corroborate your visuals. Successful visuals stand alone; the presenter shouldn't hold them. They should have titles, and any outlines or graphics should be clear and accessible to the audience. Keep your visuals simple, clear, and colorful. Use ample space; if you employ slides or an overhead projector, use the upper two-thirds of the screen. We will discuss these techniques further in Chapter 5, under "Graphics."

After you've discussed the specifics and have pointed out the connections between the general information presented in the overview, your summary should begin.

Summary

Indicate to your audience that you are summarizing. Begin with phrases such as: "In summary," or "In conclusion," or "To summarize." This signals the audience that you are concluding and that they should be especially attentive.

A summary should reflect information provided in the overview. An effective way to conclude the presentation is to revisit the visuals used in the overview. This is a clear and simple way to tie a presentation together. No new information, nor details or points not previously mentioned should be given in a summary. You should mention or list salient points so as to give a strong and confident support to your ideas. For instance:

In closing, we have the three focal points of a presentation: the overview, the body, and the summary.

1. *The Overview* — the title in general terms, the big picture, how and what is going to be presented and by whom; also, do not be afraid of a dramatic opening: Example: smashing an inferior product with a hammer to demonstrate your product's resilience.
2. *The Body* — the specifics; the details supporting, defining, and explaining the general terms introduced in the overview.
3. *The Summary* — the tying together of a presentation's purpose; connecting specific terms with the general terms; emphasizing key points and explaining possible outcomes/results related to this presentation.

Following these three points will ensure a focused, effective presentation.

Now a few post-presentation questions should be asked:

1. Did you address your purpose and the audience's needs?
2. Is there a need for follow-up information (such as handouts) or future presentations?
3. Did you meet your expectations for this presentation? (Do not be overly critical; presenting is a developmental process.)
4. What supportive and corrective feedback can you offer yourself?

Often after making a presentation we are more than ready to critique ourselves. We think, "I should have done this . . ." or "I should have done that . . ." when, in fact, no one knew what you were going to do or say except for you. Many presenters are much too critical of themselves.

At the top of a blank sheet of paper write "supportive feedback," and on the other side, write "corrective feedback." When you critique yourself, you should analyze feedback, from yourself and others, under these two categories: supportive feedback provides reinforcement for what you did well, for areas where little change is necessary, and corrective feedback, which suggests alternatives, or ways to improve how or what you presented. Don't be too critical; make sure you list feedback under both headings.

Any presenter can apply this presentation design to any content area. Feel free to delete or interchange any of the design concepts. The purpose of this design is to accomplish your presentation objectives, rather than an exact replica of the design structure.

PRESENTATION CONTENT MODEL

Collect Information

- Pre-presentation; ask the right questions.
- Make the presentation; focus on your purpose and respond to the audience's needs, keeping in mind the sophistication of the audience.
- After the presentation, take follow-up action; provide handouts, schedule future presentations; present more details or new information.

Support Information

- Design visuals (graphics, bullet points).
- Explain and support what you showed the audience.
- Give the audience options as to how to understand your points (visual, verbal, tactile, possibly smell and taste).
- Models or product examples are very helpful.

Presentation Design

- Plan for the desired climate (tone, or mind set) of the presentation (examples: friendly and relaxed; professional and structured; authoritative; sales pitch, etc.).

- Organize and sequence the material to create the flow that you want.
- Create a method of follow-up; ask yourself, "Who is going to interpret and apply the material I've presented?" Plan for follow-up.

Presentation Format Review

- Overview
- Greeting/Introduction
- Title of presentation
- Objectives:
    — Why are you presenting?

    — What do you want to accomplish?

    — Who is the audience (sophisticated, naive)?

    — What is in it for the audience? (What are the benefits of listening to this presentation?)
- Be dramatic. Give a demonstration. Show a product. Smash a product!
- Statement opener; use a sentence that is a thought-provoker, a grabber, such as: "Before you leave you will be a million dollars wiser. Why?"
- Set the ground rules: questions and answers, handouts, time limit, breaks, small group interaction, audience interaction (anything else).

Building Your Presentation

- What is this presentation going to cover?
- Highlight topics or main points (visuals are helpful).

Daydream, formulate ideas, write a theme, write general topics, and outline your thoughts into an overview, body, and summary.

Overview

The overview should inform the audience of all the topics to be presented and the analytical facts to be discussed. The process by which the audience is expected to respond, such as asking questions or sharing their own experiences, should be explained. After the overview, there should be no surprises concerning what is to be presented.

Body

The body of the presentation should flow smoothly from the overview. Discuss your ideas with the audience. Let your personality and style come across. Be yourself. Do not "read" a presentation. The body should be logically organized and engaging. Note cards with topic sentences will help you keep your thoughts (and the presentation) on track. Visual aids should be used for support. Slides, overheads, and flip charts are most beneficial to audience comprehension.

Back up specific details (visual and verbal) on each of the topics or main points with supportive material. Provide pictures of the product's process (before, during, after), service, policies, rules and procedures, etc. Reminder: Pictures of end products build credibility and excitement. If you produce car bumpers, show the bumpers on a car, not just the bumpers.

Summary

Let the audience know when you're summarizing. Bridge the specific "In summary . . ." with the overview (often the overview material can be used again). Emphasize key points and follow-up reading—set time frames for use or suggestions. The summary should reinforce the salient ideas of the presentation. It also should include questions directed to the audience regarding the main topics of the presentation and a recapping of key issues by the audience with your guidance. The summary should be brief and present concepts or issues that you want the audience to contemplate. Remind the audience of the benefits of listening to your presentation.

Follow-up

Outline the presentation or highlighted points. Indicate what is next. What are the objectives following the presentation? Set dates for follow-up.

WAYS TO BUILD RAPPORT

1. Draw people into the discussion (audience participation). Use a name card in front of each participant and call on each by name. For a large audience, this method might be awkward; ask general questions instead. Have members of the audience relate their experiences. Respond to nonverbal gestures and facial expressions that indicate the person understands what you want. Ask questions and provide answers. Then, ask the audience, "Has this happened to you . . . ?" or "Have you used . . . ?" or "Have you thought about . . . ?" Talk to the people who respond.
2. Be "other-directed." Think about the audience's interests. Present what they came to hear on a level of comprehension suitable to them.
3. Create interest via your voice and visuals. Vary your rate of speech to reflect your message. Concentrate on your vocal inflection as a means of creating excitement. Make eye contact with participants as you move around the room or platform.
4. Know the subject. Be aware of any new research information on the subject and present it proficiently. Do not read your presentation.
5. Be careful about asking if there are any questions. By asking for a volunteer you are asking if anyone wants to take a risk. Refer to point 1. Ask and answer questions of yourself. This is a way to begin the question and answers—it might break down some barriers.

Now try to apply some of the principles we've discussed. The following is a case study of a presentation problem for you to analyze. Read the case, and then answer the questions that follow.

The Case of the Frustrating Business Presentation

Joe was asked to give a presentation at the yearly sales meeting this year. Joe has been a salesman at the Miracle Company (MC) for fifteen years. He knows the products extremely well and his customers like him. He has studied the products and can explain them in great detail. Because he had an outstanding year, he was asked to present. His manager, Bill, who has been with the company two years, is a quiet but likable man. Joe does not seem to get his ideas across to Bill. When they have business meetings, Joe presents what he has done. Inevitably, Bill follows up the meeting with a memo telling Joe he needs more information.

During the yearly sales meeting, Joe presented the workings of the products and his thoughts on why the MC products are superior to those of his competitors. He did not address the business objectives. Bill had said he wanted to know the sales quotients to follow up on his presentation. Joe did not present that information. Bill told Joe that his presentation was not complete. Joe said, "I have put hours into gathering information from customers and other sales and marketing people to put this presentation together." Joe said, in a huff, that he needed more time to collect information about the sales of the products to satisfy Bill's request for the sales quotients.

The Initial Presentation Design

Bill is frustrated because he thinks no one understands his concerns as a manager. A manager must know the entire score of business, not just the differences between products. Joe feels frustrated because he knows the products and thinks no one cares about his fifteen years experience.

Questions

1. Who is at fault, the presenter or the listener?

   Both men are at fault for the communication gap. Neither clearly established the "why" and "what" of the presentation. A clear idea of the presentation objectives and mutual investment (or buy-in) is missing.

2. What strategy would eliminate Joe's and Bill's frustration?

   Both men should outline their respective presentations with an overview, a body, and a summary, and the focus of a possible follow-up. Clearly they need to understand the focus of the presentation.

3. Is there a lack of communication between Joe and his boss?

   Joe and Bill have to communicate on mutual terms and be other-directed, or concerned with each other's needs. There is communication, but there is a lack of quality communication.

The bottom line here is: target your audience, the why's and what's of presenting, and the follow-up.

A presentation should target the audience's needs and desires. If a presentation does not meet business objectives, several people might be at fault. Why? Never assume people understand what you want in a presentation. Go back to the golden rule of presentation: collect, disseminate, and share information.

SUMMARY FOR DESIGNING A PRESENTATION

When preparing a presentation, several questions must be addressed:

1. Why am I speaking? What do I want to accomplish? This will give the presentation a clear purpose and direction.
2. With whom am I speaking? What is the level of the audience (naive, sophisticated, unknown, or mixed)? By addressing these questions, the presentation will meet the comprehension level or expectations of the audience. What kind of presentation will meet the audience's expectations: persuasive or informative?
3. How long should I talk? It is important to meet the presenter's and the audience's expectation of time. A few minutes one way or another is not crucial, but an hour over is deadly. A presentation should be flexibly structured. Stay within the time frame, but don't end abruptly because your time is up.

The Initial Presentation Design 41

4. How should the presentation be outlined? There are several factors to consider when structuring a presentation:

   a. *Overview* — title, general terms, big picture, what is going to be presented.

   b. *Body* — specific terms, details, and supporting, defining, and explaining the general terms.

   c. *Summary* — the tying together of the presentation purpose, application of the specific terms with the general terms, emphasizing key points, and explaining possible outcome results related to this presentation.

   d. *Post-presentation Questions* — did you address the audience's needs? Is there a need for follow-up? Did you meet your expectations for this presentation?

Preparing a successful presentation means asking the right questions before you give the answers. We all know the answers. We have been educated, trained, nurtured, and forced to give answers. However, an effective presentation must begin by asking the right questions.

CHAPTER 4

PRESENTMENT: THE BIG PICTURE

> *"It's interesting to trace the diffusion of ideas around the world. Something germinates in one place and is carried to another place largely by the accident of human contact. Like seeds borne in the fur of wandering animals, ideas often pass from person to person and from culture to culture. The channels of commerce have for many years provided an infrastructure for the movement of ideas."*
>
> *(Albrecht and Zemke, 1985, p. 19)*

Presentment, not just content, is the message. How you present is as important as what you present. Your tone, appearance, and enthusiasm create the environment in which your words are interpreted. As Malcolm Knowles would say, "This is setting the climate."

Many years of schooling and experience in a specific area do not ensure the ability to explain a particular topic. An individual can thoroughly examine a subject and be well-versed in the modern techniques of that particular field, yet find it difficult to adequately present that material to a group. The ability to remember facts and figures doesn't ensure that you can present the content in an informative and interesting manner.

A presenter's format and enthusiasm can greatly influence an audience's comprehension of the subject. The same information, presented by two different people, might be interpreted differently due to the style of each presenter. Your presentment skills can shape the audience's interpretation and sway their opinion.

Thus, it is important to present information logically and enthusiastically. Presentations do not have to be boring to be informative; a speaker's excitement can effectively aid a factual presentation. The emotions evoked during presentations can influence the audience's attitudes. The audience remembers liking or disliking the speaker (and this image rests heavily on the presentation style), and the information presented. Thus, the speaker's impression indirectly becomes part of the audience's motivation for or against the message.

Interest in a subject is nurtured through exciting, thought-provoking presentations. Therefore, realize that the shape of the presentation should be based not only on what information is given to the audience, but also on how it is given to the audience.

SUMMARY CHECKLIST FOR PRESENTATION

The following points will help you build interest in a presentation. While some of these ideas should be familiar by now, consider them in terms of presentment, or the impression the speaker creates:

1. As the presenter, you should appear competent. You should be able to present both the background and the newest concepts (or facts) on the subject matter. It is paramount that you know your subject matter, but not in a memorized fashion. You should develop a general knowledge of a specific area and be able to explain, analyze, apply, and evaluate all of the facts you present. Talking and explaining the subject matter as if you are chatting with a colleague is appealing to the audience, and it encourages rapport between them and you. As a presenter, you should start with an overview of general concepts and systematically explain the specifics until you are satisfied that all of the content has been discussed.

2. You should know in advance what the audience expects from your presentation. If you do not know what the audience expects, elicit questions to generate participation. Remain flexible to the audience's needs. Research the needs of the audience by speaking with an informed source prior to the discussion.

3. In the allotted period of time only a certain amount of content can be presented. You should prepare for the presentation by outlining all the major concepts you wish to cover. Note

cards are a good way to identify topic sentences and important points, but they should act only as an outline to your discussion. Presentations should rarely be read. In a quality presentation, the speaker emphasizes salient facts and arranges them in a logical sequence to create an effective learning process during the presentation.

4. Draw the participants into the presentation with questions rather than waiting for questions. As the presenter, you should ask questions to generate dialogue. This, of course, is not a technique that works well with large audiences (150 or more). If possible, use name cards for the audience or ask participants to identify themselves by name and position before the presentation begins. If neither of these techniques are appropriate, simply point to individuals you wish to respond and draw them into a dialogue. You also can draw in audience members by having them relate experiences. Small group discussions also generate questions or solutions to problems. Do not let the audience passively sit by as you discuss ideas. How will you know what they are thinking? How will you know if they are comprehending?

5. In your role as the presenter, you act as a "visual" and should be cognizant of your movement. Nervous gestures distract from factual content (for instance, keeping your hands in your pockets and jingling change). Good posture, synchronized body movements, and eye contact greatly enhance the presenter as a visual. Similarly, a presenter's body movements can

draw the audience's attention. A presenter who wishes to appear authoritative and strong should stand. A presenter who wishes to be accepted as part of the audience or as a colleague might sit while speaking. Practice your presentation in front of a mirror; be conscious of your visual techniques.

As a visual, you should meet the audience's expectations of what a presenter should be. For instance, it is important that you dress the way the audience expects because dress and appearance can enhance your credibility as a presenter. There are no right or wrong answers to appearance; common sense is the best approach.

6. A presenter should change the pace of the presentation by varying the rate of speech. Use your voice as an instrument. To highlight different, specific, and important facts, you should speak slowly and loudly; pausing after an important thought is also effective. A presenter can create emphasis with a five-second pause, and thereby embellish a sentence. A pause, if used consciously and appropriately, is as important as the syntax of a sentence.

7. The length of the presentation should not exceed the time needed to present and recap the necessary information. Repetitive presentment may be necessary to highlight some salient points, but don't waste time. If you can conclude a presentation earlier than the allotted time, do so. You should quit before everyone knows what you are going to say next.

8. Use a brief summary to explain the overview and the specifics that were covered. The final summary is extremely important. It must pull together all the facts and create a whole concept of what was presented, rather than a group of isolated facts. A presenter should begin the summary with a brief overview, explain concepts in detail, and then summarize the salient points. After the summary, ask for questions. If you want to stimulate discussion, break the audience into small groups to analyze a topic. The audience usually does not ask questions without prompting.

These eight concepts should be used as a checklist in the preparation of a presentation. Identify your strong points as a presenter and exploit your best characteristics.

Breathing

A presenter's source of energy for speaking is proper breathing. When speaking, breathe from the diaphragm, not the upper part of your chest. Your vocal chords become tired if they are used and not supported by the diaphragm muscle. You must project your voice when you present. Breathing from the upper chest will not aid in projecting your voice. Breathing from the diaphragm gives your voice full tone without making it necessary for you to speak too loudly.

A presenter can also relax by breathing properly. Prior to presenting, regulate your breathing by inhaling to a count of four, holding for a count of four, and exhaling to a count of four. Practice this breathing pattern until it is unconsciously maintained. During the presentation, when you need to take a breath, pause and breathe. Do not try to squeeze words out as you run out of air. When you are comfortable, you are breathing properly.

General Vs. Specific Content

As stated previously, there are two ways to present ideas: generally (to describe the big picture) and specifically (analytically). Your reason for presenting an idea determines which approach is appropriate. For example, a secretary may be described by peers as having "good typing skills," a general concept. When someone recommends that same secretary for a job, it is necessary to describe such typing skills specifically, mentioning details such as speed, error rate, and technical typing ability. Likewise, a salesperson may be recognized as the "top salesperson of the month," a general description. When responding to a request for a raise, this same salesperson must be evaluated specifically: "This person sold $1,850 of material in one month—the highest amount ever sold by one salesperson in our company in a thirty-day period. In the past year, this employee consistently sold at least $1,000,000 worth of materials per month."

The manner in which information is presented (in general or specific terms) depends upon the perception level of the audience. Specific (analytical) information may be useless or boring to an audience that is not educated in the particular field addressed. For example, a chemist who has to justify research to peers needs to use chemical equations and terminologies. For the board of directors that gives the final approval for research funding, the same chemist has to use general terms to justify the research and how it will benefit the corporation. The chemist needs to use specific terms when presenting to knowledgeable peers, and general terms when presenting to those who pay the salaries but do not necessarily have strong backgrounds in chemistry.

People have unique patterns of comprehension, which originate from their use and development of their individual experiences and innate abilities. Experiences and innate abilities affect the way information is processed and, consequently, the way people respond and behave. Different people may perceive the same stimulus differently, due to their dominant brain processes, which produce individual styles of learning or understanding. For this reason it is necessary for a presentation to begin with general terms and then flow to specific terms, so that the listeners can assimilate the information according to their particular learning patterns. However, there are times when it may be more appropriate to start with specific terms and move to general terms. For example, a presentation in which the topic might be stated as "How long will it take you to market Product A?" should immediately begin with such specifics as: time, procedure, cost, demand, manufacturing, and so on. Ultimately, it is the presenter's responsibility to guide the listener toward an understanding of general and specific terms that the listener can comprehend, synthesize, and evaluate, and which serve the presenter's purposes.

As a presenter, you should know (or find out) the comprehension level of the audience. You can guide the audience from its initial level of comprehension toward an effective understanding of the presented information through the overview (general concepts), the body (specific concepts), and the summary (general and specifics). As you present, keep in mind that both you (the speaker) and the audience (listeners) have needs that must be met. Both you and the audience have unique qualities of understanding, a need to learn, and preferred modes of perceiving. You should feel fulfilled through the self-expression of your presentation, and your audience should gain a sense of fulfillment from its acquisition of desired information.

When considering a presentment style, keep in mind that:

1. Each person presenting ideas (supervisor, support staff member, salesperson, educator) has a unique mode of presentation.

2. Each person listening to or viewing the content of has a unique or particular mode of comprehension.

3. To create results that are favorable, use different modes of presenting so the audience has the freedom to choose a method of acquiring the information.

AUDIENCE INTERPRETATION MODEL

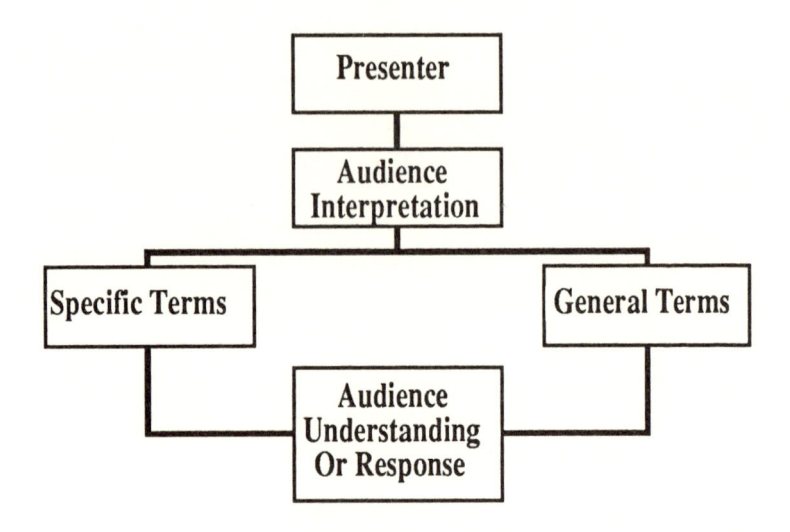

```
        ┌─────────────┐
        │  Presenter  │
        └──────┬──────┘
        ┌─────────────┐
        │   Audience  │
        │Interpretation│
        └──────┬──────┘
      ┌────────┴────────┐
┌───────────┐      ┌─────────────┐
│Specific   │      │General Terms│
│Terms      │      │             │
└─────┬─────┘      └──────┬──────┘
      │    ┌─────────────┐│
      └────┤  Audience   ├┘
           │Understanding│
           │ Or Response │
           └─────────────┘
```

Know your audience: Why are they listening? What are their listening needs? What follow-up is needed to ensure that the audience's expectations of knowing (acquiring information) are met? What concepts of understanding will the audience achieve if you present general concepts (overview) and move toward the specific? Regardless of the innate abilities of an audience, you can guide them toward your (the presenter's) level of comprehension by experiencing your presentation, and thereby reinforcing the newly learned concepts.

As a presenter, you must observe the audience for signs of comprehension. Ask questions to pinpoint salient ideas that need to be established. A listener may say, "I understand," but that does not mean that he or she understands as you intend. Present and ask general questions first. Let the audience respond. Concentrate on whether the audience responds to your questions in general or specific terms. Then, determine how you can guide the audience toward comprehension on your (the presenter's) level. You can move toward specifics by using jargon and/or diagrams.

Your completed presentation, in both general and specific terms, should provide the audience with a complete concept. An interplay between the general and specific concepts should be developed so comparisons can be made, and both the audience and you (the presenter) have choices in the asking of questions and in the follow-up.

The depth of communication is usually at the discretion of the presenter. Use common sense as to how long you should discuss an issue. If someone asks you what time it is, you should not tell the person how to build a clock. When formulating your ideas for communication (discussion, meeting, memo, phone call), keep in mind general and specific terms. Fulfill the listeners' needs while effectively communicating and meeting your needs as a presenter.

SHAPING A PRESENTATION

The brain processes new information in a 'big picture' manner. After the brain becomes familiar with the information, it will begin to process the information analytically. Therefore, to begin a presentation with very specific or analytical questions or explanations is often ineffective because the information will have to be repeated. Give the audience time to reacquaint or become familiar with the information.

Overview ➡

- Begin a Presentation
- General Terms
- Specific Terms

Body ➡

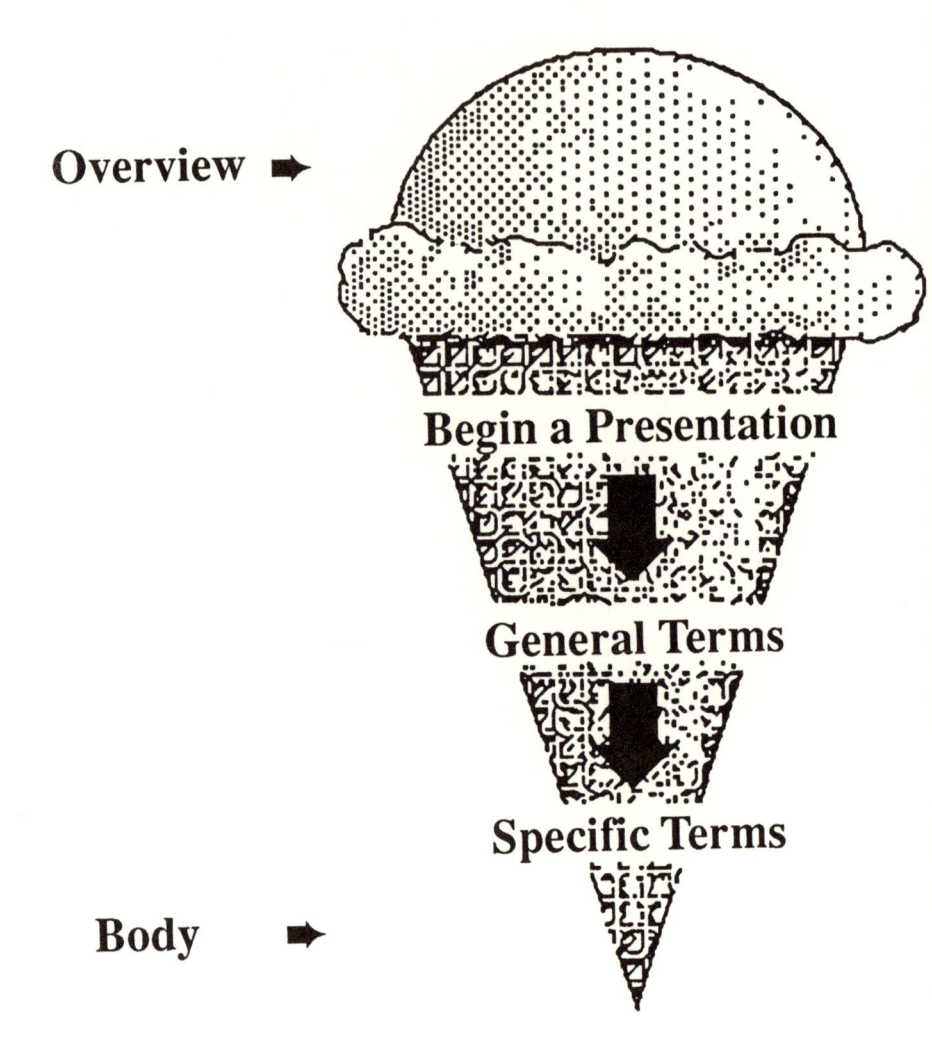

WHY AN ICE CREAM CONE?

How many people, on a hot summer day, would eat the bottom part of the cone and throw away the ice cream? Not very appetizing, is it? That is the same approach a presenter should take when introducing facts. Think of the big picture, the overview. Let the audience know what flavor the ice cream is. Does it have nuts or chocolate chips? Give the audience the overview; give them reason to make an emotional investment, then focus their attention toward the facts.

In this way, the presenter becomes a conduit between the big picture (general terms) and the analytical facts (specific terms). Of course, there are some exceptions to this construction. What do you want to accomplish? If you want to address a specific problem or need, then begin with specifics and move toward a general overview (big picture). Start at the bottom of the cone and work up, but don't present the facts without letting the audience know the benefits or applications of those facts. Offer that opportunity for emotional investment even if you save the big picture until last.

Have you ever listened to a presenter and wondered, "So what?" or "What can I do with this information?" "Now what do I do?" "How does this fit with what we do?" When you present, think of the ice cream cone. Give an overview and the facts, then guide the listeners into understanding why they are listening and how they might apply the information you offer.

Stop reading for a moment and reflect on the metaphors used thus far. Listeners will remember metaphors long after the content is forgotten. The steak, the artist's canvas, and the ice cream cone all conjure up concepts of presentation.

By now your design process should include these questions: Who is the audience? How might they process information? If your audience is a group that works together often, what traditions and standards do they have?

For example, a group of vice presidents may want an overview of the information, then the benefits, without ever going into great detail or specifics during the body of a presentation. If you are presenting to a group of visiting executives, what good will hours of details do them? Ask the right questions for your audience before you inundate them with answers, such as facts, conclusions, or results that do not interest them.

Take this opportunity to daydream by using the reflection model. It asks questions, helps you develop strategy or a method of design that helps you act, present, then helps you reassess what you did by offering supportive and corrective feedback.

Read the Reflection Model and think about a presentation. Then read the Reflection Model again.

Concept/Goal

Title your presentation. Consider why and what are you presenting, and what are the desired results.

Reflect

Outline your ideas, collect materials, focus on presenting these in a way that will achieve your results.

Act

Present, and keep in mind that a presentation continues as long as people reflect on what you are presenting.

Reassess

Critique yourself, but don't be too critical; analyze your strengths as well as any areas that need improvement or alternative concepts.

Always consider reflection and presentation as ongoing processes.

PRESENTATION IS A ONE-ON-ONE EXPERIENCE

We are unique individuals with certain idiosyncrasies that affect our presentment and listening. Both innate abilities and environmental experiences contribute to the way people interact. As a presenter, it is important that you understand this concept and recognize that several modes of presentment are necessary if you want to meet the varied needs and learning styles of your listeners. Even though a speaker usually addresses a group of people, presentation is a one-to-one experience. Let's examine this concept.

As the presenter, it is your job to guide the audience toward a common understanding. A speaker accomplishes this goal by presenting well-organized material in several ways, each at the audience's level of comprehension, moving listeners to a mutual and new level of comprehension.

Visual imagery, such as pictures, graphics, and diagrams supersedes all other modes of presentment. People have said, "a picture's worth a thousand words" for centuries, and there's a reason for that. Most of what we retain mentally we receive through our eyes. People remember information longer if it is received visually as well as aurally. The recipient of visual information can review material and experiences at a controlled pace. When people must listen predominantly, they must comprehend at the pace the speaker sets. A presenter should create silent time for the receiver when presenting a visual. Use this same "silent" technique when demonstrating or distributing products or handouts. Give your audience a chance to take in the information.

For example: When you use overhead transparencies, do not immediately begin explaining the image. Show the visual, then wait for your audience to study it. Watch a few faces. When people finish examining or reading the material, they will break eye contact with the visual and return their attention to you. Although aural and visual experiences complement each other, it is very difficult to use both simultaneously. Try to spell Pittsburgh and write California at the same time. It is just as difficult to read

Presentment: The Big Picture 59

(or closely examine a graphic) while someone is speaking.

Personality, for both the speaker and the listener, is integral to both learning patterns and presentment styles; it cannot be separated from what one presents and learns, or how one presents and learns. You must be aware of the ways your personality influences your own learning and presentment styles. Similarly, it's important to recognize your style of presenting and your style of listening. Each role plays a part in creating that one-to-one dynamic that enhances a presentation.

It is important to note that a person's characteristics can—and do—change according to the content addressed. As an example, compare a chemist and a musician: Although the chemist is very analytical in chemistry, he may speak in very general terms when discussing music. However, when a musician discusses music, she typically uses very specific terms. We are all potentially analytical, structure-oriented, and concrete; or general, random, and abstract, given the right material. However, the presenter must ask which style is appropriate for the listener. Again: Who is the audience? What do you want to accomplish as a presenter? What might the audience gain if they listen to, and internalize, what you have to say?

Much has been written about left or right brain dominance and its role in comprehension, and many studies on whether learning is influenced more by innate ability or environmental experiences have been conducted as well. Apparently, innate ability and environmental experiences are equally important. Educational environments usually encourage the use of the left hemispheric functions, through the development of logical, sequential, and rational thought. Most environments don't encourage the participants to actually apply or experience the knowledge they acquire. Indeed, many studies suggest that high school students who are creative problem-solvers were often the disorganized daydreamers who did not perform well in elementary school.

Again: You, as a presenter, must realize that everyone has a unique learning style, and that various presentment techniques can be utilized in developing a common understanding of information among your audience.

A summary explanation of these concepts are expressed in the "Cognitive Model" on the following page.

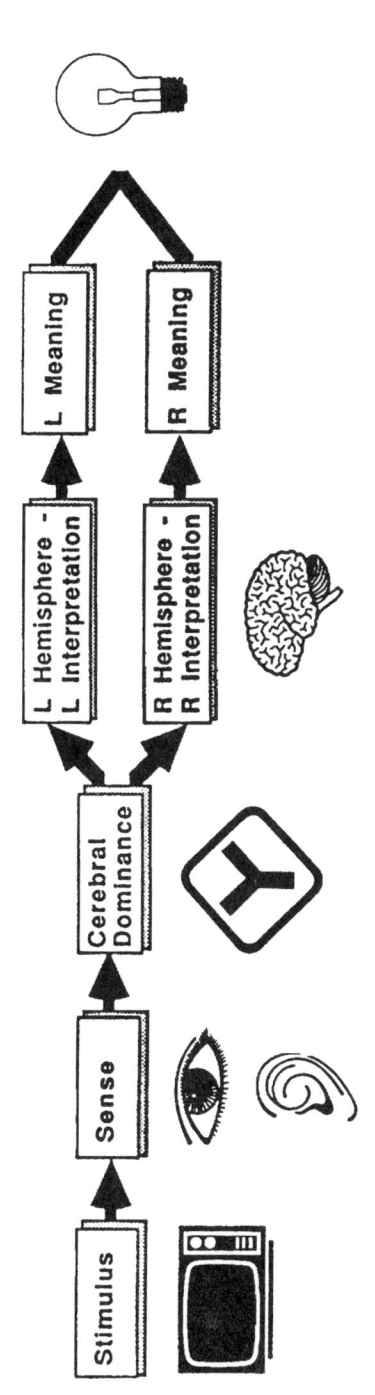

COGNITIVE MODEL

THINKING		**FEELING**
knowing	....	responding
applying	....	commitment
analyzing	....	organizing
evaluating	....	becoming

COMMUNICATION STYLES

Effective communication plays a large part in creating a mutual understanding between the presenter and the listener(s). When you are speaking, it is essential to use different communication styles. A presenter's communication styles should be flexible enough to meet the situation, and sufficiently "other directed" to acknowledge and meet the listeners' needs.

J. Brewer developed an assessment instrument, "My Best Communication," that evaluates four communication styles. The following is an adaptation.

FOUR STYLES OF COMMUNICATION

1. Bold Style

This communicator appears in charge; the person likes to be challenged by the material and the audience; usually effective at visualizing the "big picture," might not be as effective on how to make it happen. This speaker is often a poor listener. The advantage of this style is that you quickly give out and respond to information.

Thought: Consider that some people may interpret this style as uncaring and impersonal. This communicator is a poor listener, moving on to other points often and without letting others finish their statement. When using this style, make an effort to concentrate on what is said. You may want to take notes, which will ensure that you accurately collect information and keep you from responding too quickly.

2. Expressive Style

This speaker is a persuader; likes popularity, usually relates well to people and sometimes talks too much. The advantage to this style is that it allows quite a bit of information to be disseminated within a given time frame. The question: Is it all necessary?

Thought: When speaking, know what you want to say, and don't repeat yourself or oversell your point. Create a structure; write notes or an agenda and stick to it. Don't embellish or editorialize your content.

3. Sympathetic Style

This presenter likes to be a member of the group; requires personal attention from the members of the audience and is quickly "turned off" by aggressiveness; usually likes to listen more than talk. The advantage of this style is an awareness of communication dynamics and uses them well; most successful when presenting to a small group that needs and shares personal attention.

Thought: When using this style, try not to feel "put off" or affronted if others are brief, or if they ask you to move quickly through your information.

4. Technical Style

This speaker is thorough and detail-oriented; may overlook the people side of presentation; likes low-risk situations to ponder any questions or responses offered. The advantage of this style is that it omits very little information from the presentation. The question: Does the audience need all the information provided?

Thought: If you depend on this style, take time to simplify your content occasionally, so your audience gets the big picture instead of great detail; too many details often confuse the issue rather than clarifying it.

Everyone exhibits some traits of each style or characteristics in their individual behavior. A good presenter must recognize which traits are dominant in a given situation. While functioning in the working environment, a person may be objective, unfeeling, and quick to make a decision. However, in the family environment, that same person may be empathetic, understanding, and slow to make decisions concerning the family's future and needs.

If one person describes the style or traits of someone you know, you may be surprised at the portrayal; perhaps you relate with that "someone" in an environment that the describer hasn't experienced.

We've all described friends as having different "sides" to their personalities. Another example: I have a friend who will not telephone me at work, because she says she hates my "work voice." A skillful presenter draws on different traits when presenting, especially when a specific environment or audience "needs" or "expects" a particular style. People change—sometimes within the same presentation—according to the content and its application or use, according to their time and needs, to their background knowledge of a subject, and according to a bias toward/against the presenter.

The goal of understanding and analyzing different communication styles is not to become a psychologist, but to more effectively and productively interact with other people; to acknowledge and respond to their unique perceptions and needs. Keep in mind that different people will treat you in various ways. There's nothing wrong with your personal style, but you must begin analyzing situations as your style and personality relate to them; you must respond to others according to their styles, because people will not, and often cannot, immediately respond to you on your level.

Thus careful consideration must be given to the styles or traits apparent in your listeners. If both you and your listener choose to be judgmental, and if you disagree on a decision, an argument may result. If you are sensing and listening while your partner is intuitive, then you are looking for facts while your partner is feeling or imagining a bigger picture or possibly some future situation.

Use your presentation skills to motivate your audience. Make your communication style attractive to them, and make clear what they might gain by listening to you.

Summary

Outline to Enhancing Presentment Skills

Communication

1. Create a clear understanding for yourself and the audience.
2. Present for your audience, not for yourself.
3. Be trusting and sincere.
4. Use different modes of presentment (visuals, explanation, diagrams, small group discussions, etc.).
5. Present a logical overview, move from general to specifics, then recap.
6. Generate the emotional level needed to create enthusiasm for the presentation.
7. Anticipate the audience's reactions.

Listening Skills

1. Listen without rebuttal and concentrate on what is being said.
2. Respond to what is said, not to what you think should be said. Be direct.
3. Write words or comments (flip charts, overheads) to focus visually on a specific concept.

Organization Skills

1. Establish and prioritize the expected results of your presentation.
2. Identify the methods and actions that will achieve the expected results.
3. Know why you are speaking about this topic.
4. Set a logical time frame for the presentation in order to achieve the results you expect.
5. Apply your presentation skills to a presentation format.
6. Reassess your thoughts and actions.

Contemplate what motivates. What are the motives and purposes of your listeners? The listener's interest must be reinforced with the benefits you offer.

In order to establish an effective presentation/communication style, a presenter must realize that people perceive differently. In addition, you should identify what perceptions dominate your own learning and communicating paths, and you must keep in mind that others may not share your perceptions. Whenever you present, address the audience's concerns and perceptual strengths.

Use visual and verbal methods for collecting, sharing, and disseminating information. When it's feasible, appeal to your audience's tactile sense as well. Question your audience and encourage them to ask questions. Often you can paraphrase the audience's questions to create a focused understanding.

Reflect upon your usual style of perceiving information, based on your response to the inventory questions. Effective presenters are "other directed". Ask yourself, "Who will interpret my thoughts when I leave, and how might they do it?" Be proactive in establishing follow-up feedback through handouts. Use creative visual and verbal communications; any method of presentment (visual, verbal, or some combination of the senses) is successful if it achieves your intended goals.

A presentation has two distinct functions: (1) to collect, disseminate, and share information and (2) to create an "emotional investment" that encourages the audience to use or to apply concepts from your presentation. Help the audience to know why your information is important. Guide them toward a clear and mutual understanding of your thoughts from a point of view that includes factual information, the audience's needs or desires, and an application of your ideas.

By clearly helping the audience understand and apply concepts from your presentation, you enhance your skills as a presenter and provide benefits to the audience. This focus on the audience's needs and perceptions will also ensure that your presentation takes place as a "one-to-one" relationship, and that your presentation will continue after you leave. According to Skinner (1976), "to experience the world is to test it, and to perceive it is to capture it." It is your job to perceive and capture your audience; if you succeed, they will capture your ideas.

CHAPTER 5

PRESENTMENT: THE ESSENTIAL ELEMENTS

"Many people have rich and deeply textured agendas, but without communication nothing will be realized. The management of meaning, mastery of communication, is inseparable from effective leadership."

(Bennis, 1985, p. 33)

PLAN TO MEET AUDIENCE NEEDS

To be an effective presenter you must meet the needs of your audience, and you can best address their needs by continually being other-directed: by sharing, disseminating, and collecting information in a manner that constitutes an effective presentation.

Your audience should be involved in the presentation process, but this doesn't mean that you should allow them to control the flow of the presentation by continually asking questions. As a presenter, you should elicit audience participation. You can involve audience members by asking open-ended questions and by giving them time to respond mentally. In addition, you might provide a worksheet on ways to apply the presented information. If it is feasible, let your listeners form groups and discuss any notable issues, ways they might apply the presented information, or questions they may have.

If you involve audience members in the presentation process, there is a greater chance that they will apply the information they receive. Audience involvement also permits members to assume various active roles—such as explaining material or their own experiences, questioning the presenter, and challenging their colleagues. This allows participants to be active, rather than approaching the subject with an attitude that says, "Here I am; entertain and stimulate me."

When people interact in a group they tend to assume different roles. When presenting, you must identify your role within this interaction, whether you act as a questioner, explainer, researcher, or some combination of these, the audience will more readily assume these roles themselves. Your role as a presenter is multifaceted because audience members view you in different ways: helper, problem-solver, colleague, scapegoat, expert, and so on. Ultimately, your role expands well beyond the time you spend presenting to include the listeners' reflections and applications of the material you've presented. Caution: In no circumstances should you assume the role of "attacker," nor should you allow members of the group to assume that role. An attacker is a person who "name calls," or personally disparages another person. If a presentation ever reaches the point when its participants communicate by attacking each other, information is no longer the dominant issue, and the presenter has lost control. When the presenter focuses the audience's energies toward results or outcomes, everyone involved in the presentation, speaker and audience, will benefit. But no benefits result when a group squanders its energy and attention on personal attacks.

Presenters must develop a plan that will guide the audience's energies toward fulfilling their goals. As stated in Chapter 2, knowing technical data is not enough; an effective presenter transcends technical data to establish a level of comprehension that is accessible to the audience.

Follow-up is used to ensure the audience's compliance to or application of the presented information. It is an essential, yet difficult aspect of a presentation. Remember that your presentation begins before you arrive and continues after you have gone. You should identify your audience and anticipate their expectations before your presentation. One way to accomplish this audience profile includes telephoning a colleague or a member of the audience and asking what they expect. The better prepared you are for the presentation, the less anxiety you will feel, because you have eliminated part of the unknown. If you are well prepared, the presentation should be easy, and you can use this opportunity to express your thoughts. As a presenter, you become a catalyst; for instance, you can constructively create agreement, or disagreement, while stimulating the audience's thought process.

In planning your presentation, consider the equipment you intend to use. As always, Murphy's Law prevails: If something can go wrong, it will. Try to anticipate any potential problems, and keep the essential audiovisual and organizational portions of your presentation with you.

Questions: When preparing for a presentation, consider why the audience members are there, what their expectations are, why you are presenting, and how you can ensure the utilization of the presented information. This section identifies interaction roles, suggests ways to deal with questions raised during your presentation, and describes the various influences that may affect your audience.

THE TWO SIDES OF A PRESENTATION

There are two sides to a presentation: content or technical knowledge (content side), and audience involvement (people side). Keep in mind that the listeners' perception of your content and their "emotional investment" in the information occur simultaneously. Emotional investment includes reading, reflecting upon, discussing, showing interest in, or listening to the presentation. You must know the content, what you're presenting, and the presentation process to be used. As you share information, your listeners perceive the technical content and digest it, because they are emotionally involved in the presentation.

A presenter should take nothing for granted. Many times presenters present, then analyze their performance without clearly thinking of what should be accomplished. This is not the way to plan an effective presentation.

An effective presenter plans and anticipates the presentation. The following model describes this outcome of the process.

TWO SIDES OF PRESENTATION MODEL

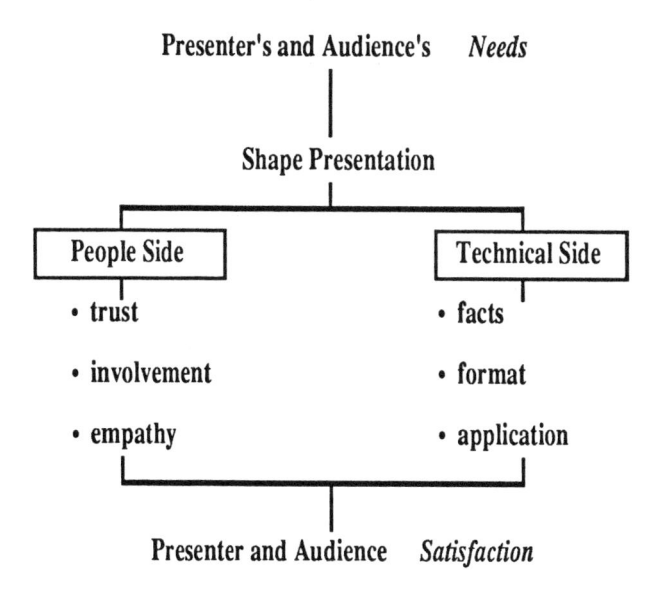

Presenter's and Audience's *Needs*

Shape Presentation

People Side	Technical Side
• trust	• facts
• involvement	• format
• empathy	• application

Presenter and Audience *Satisfaction*

Given the audience, the time of day, the length of your presentation, the type of presentation (for instance, persuasive or informative), and the goals you must accomplish, you also must identify your content and the process you will use to build a satisfactory presentation. In other words, a presenter should envision what specifically must occur to ensure anticipated results, and what specific actions or presentation techniques are needed to meet expectations. In addition, two other factors—audience need and involvement—must be addressed as well.

To meet expectations the presenter should focus on how to build a technically sound presentation, and on how to involve the audience. The following points present a dichotomy of a presentation by analyzing technical knowledge (content) correlated with suggestions on how to involve an audience.

ANALYSIS OF THE VERBAL PRESENTATION

People interact differently because of the various roles they assume in conversation. If you are aware of the roles available to the audience, you will respond more effectively to your needs and your audience's needs. As a presenter/listener, you should utilize each of the following interaction roles (except for attacking).

Pausing Utilize silence: words are interwoven on a background of silence; thus, it is an element of speaking. Use pauses to emphasize and clarify your ideas.

Explaining	Describe something; tell, as needed; disseminate information.
Paraphrasing	Reiterate, restate, and clarify information offered by others as well as your own points; mirror the words that were stated. This lets the questioner hear what was said. Many times people do not listen to themselves. They are thinking of their next thoughts. This role is particularly essential in phone presentations.
Questioning	Ask questions; get a better understanding of the information or feedback your audience offers.
Listening	Collect, interpret, and incorporate the information audience members offer.
Feeling	Express an effective opinion ("I feel that . . . ."); share information, use your sensitivity to help you understand what is said.
Reinforcing	Offer support; use phrases like "I agree with that because . . . ."
Relating	Tell a story; relate your own experiences; use metaphors and analogies.
Challenging	Disagree intellectually; discuss an argumentative point. Keep in

	mind, however, that there is risk involved in challenging a listener with your point of view.
Humoring	Break the ice; you might tell a joke, but be careful. Do not open your presentation with a joke. People aren't bored in the beginning. Plan your humor to enter the presentation naturally.
Interjecting	Politely interrupt (say, "Excuse me, but . . . ."); you might touch the arm of the speaker to establish contact. Caution: Some people may not accept interruption or physical contact. Break eye contact with the listener; draw other people in for support by looking at them. Closing the distance can be a very useful technique. Walk closer to the person; your eye contact is stronger and you will be better able to control the discussion. If possible, write what the person stated before you interject; use the visual as support.
Attacking	Avoid at all costs. This is a personal, verbal assault on a person with little regard for facts; this should not be used, except as a venting process. When attacking occurs the presentation has stopped.

Consider these questions: Who controls a conversation, the speaker, the listener, or both? What roles do you typically use while giving a presentation? It has often been said that :

'intelligent people talk about concepts'. They:
- Explain
- Paraphrase
- Question
- Challenge
- Reinforce

while *'mediocre people talk about things'*. They:
- Relate
- Humor
- Feel

and *'fools talk about other people'*. They:
- Attack

Now consider these questions: Who is in control of a conversation (a group interaction)? Who is the most authoritative person? The loudest? The most knowledgeable? Why?

You, as the presenter, should be in control of your presentation. Even while an audience member asks a question or contributes an experience, you should control or focus this exchange by establishing eye contact with the speaker; by standing and gesturing to assert your own role in the exchange; and by responding intellectually.

What role do you usually assume in a presentation? Why? Is it appropriate?

As a presenter, you inevitably assume some role or relationship with your audience. Are you there to inform or influence? How will the audience perceive your presence, and how can you influence their understanding of you?

> *"Communication, this property has to do with how well group members are understanding one another—how clearly they are communicating their ideas, values, and feelings. Even nonverbal communication can often be eloquent. A person's posture, facial expression, and gestures, tell a great deal about what he is thinking and feeling."*
>
> *(Knowles, 1972, p. 45)*

All of these questions will help you define and understand your role. In addition, they can help you understand and control your influence over the audience.

EFFECTIVE LISTENING

Effective listening is an essential part of quality communication. One individual must effectively present information while another individual must listen effectively if they are to communicate. To collect information, a person must listen and adapt to the speaker's presentment style, because each person has a different style of speaking and listening. When an individual speaks, people are influenced by what is said, who is speaking and in what manner, and by the context—when, where, and why—in which the person speaks. These factors alter the listener's acceptance, perception, and interpretation of what is said. People develop different styles of speaking and listening through education, experience, and by what they expect of the communication environment.

There is no one way to effectively speak or listen. The environment and circumstances surrounding the people attempting to communicate greatly influence the level of effective communication that can occur.

Sometimes people hear most clearly what they want to hear, and sometimes they mentally cut a speaker off in mid-sentence. When speaking of presentation, we might use the adage: "If you want someone to hear you, you've got to get his attention." How might a presenter catch listeners' attention and gain some control over their exchange? Depending on the circumstances and surroundings, anything might be appropriate: yelling, speaking softly, nodding your head, using hand movements, and so on.

Listening and speaking are equally important to achieving effective communication. As we discussed earlier, communication serves three basic purposes: to disseminate, share, and collect information. The effective listener collects information, with as little bias as possible, in the manner it is presented. Ideally, information is first interpreted on the speaker's terms (What exactly was said?), and then on the listener's terms. A mutual understanding of terms should be the primary goal of communication; both participants are working to establish a shared level of comprehension.

Imagine a telegraph company: The whole concept would be useless if one built only a transmitting station and no receiving station. The purpose of effectively speaking and listening is to establish a rapport, to shape an interaction (like a presentation) that creates partners, a speaker and a listener in communion. A successful presenter strives to say, "I understand it as you understand it," rather than, "This is what you mean to say, right?" Intimidation can kill communication.

Consider your own attitude toward your content and your audience as you study the following notes:

- If you are filled with conviction, will you have room for openness? Note that when listeners have reached a conclusion, sometimes they will raise a hand, or say, "Okay," or "All right," or they may try to interrupt. Listen to what the speaker says. Many question-and-answer periods entice the listener to respond without letting the presenter finish.

- Separate what is said from who said it and his/her manner of speaking. Many times we are influenced not by a speaker's content, but by flashy delivery, our relationship with the speaker (friend, enemy, boss?), and the skill of the speaker. Sometimes great ideas are lost because the presenter did not capture the listener's attention.

  Identify your biases and be aware of them when you listen. Do not let friendship or dislikes influence your ability to carefully hear and interpret what is said.

- Listen without rebuttal, and respond to the speaker. Keep in mind that you can listen, read, or plan your answer, but you cannot do all three simultaneously. No one can comprehensively both read and listen to someone speaking. If you are formulating a rebuttal, you are not listening to what is being said.
- You know the answers. Have you stopped to identify the "right questions"? Reflect on asking pertinent questions that focus or direct communication toward your goals.
- Communication is a key that fits many locked doors. Addressing and discussing obstacles is the most efficient way to remove them. Effective communication among a group of people results in focused and directed energy.

Effective listening includes receiving and interpreting verbal information; a good listener develops an understanding of what is said without allowing the speaker's identity or manner to overly influence concepts. A good listener seeks to establish a mutual understanding with the speaker and tries to determine what response or follow-up action is appropriate, given the context of their communication.

There is no one way to listen or take in information. What is appropriate for the circumstances? What is appropriate for you? Ask yourself these questions:

1. After listening, are you quick to respond?
2. After listening, do you reflect on what was said?
3. When listening, do you form your answer before the speaker concludes?

4. Do you influence the speaker with facial expressions?
5. Do you listen to, and analyze, what is said?
6. When appropriate, do you listen and contemplate how to apply what is being said?
7. If you like the speaker, does that affect the message you hear?
8. If you dislike the speaker, does that affect the message you hear?
9. Which influences your thoughts more: the content or its presentment?
10. Do visuals (graphics) add to your comprehension?
11. Are you aware of your role as the receiver of information (supporter, rejector, friend, peer, manager, etc.)?
12. When you listen to someone, do you maintain eye contact?
13. After listening to someone, or reading a memo, do you immediately ask any questions you may have?
14. When someone is speaking, do you nod your head or use hand gestures that could affect what the person says?
15. After listening, if appropriate, do you daydream of ways to creatively apply what was said?

16. When listening, do you try to draw broad meanings (the big picture effect) from the information?

Listening is:

>**collecting** (receiving) and
>
>**interpreting information** (perceiving)
>
>to create **follow-up** (meaningful application).

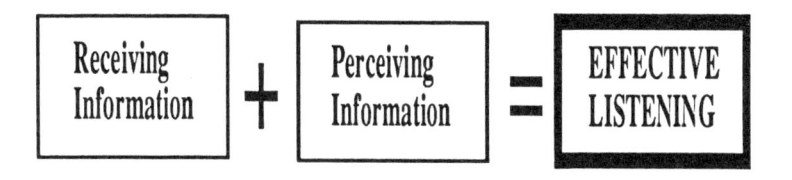

| Receiving Information | + | Perceiving Information | = | **EFFECTIVE LISTENING** |

Characteristics of Listening

Analytical	*"The data show . . . ."* This style breaks the information into parts and analyzes it.
General Terms	*"The whole idea is to . . . ."* This style presents information in broad terms.
Applicative	*"This information can be used when . . . ."* This style recognizes and points out ways the information can be used.
Innovative	*"That gives me an idea . . . ."* This style focuses on using the

	information to generate new ideas.
Enthusiastic	*"That's a great idea...."* This style helps the speaker feel accepted and underscores the listener's interest.
Friendly	*"You're my friend...."* This style suggests that friends always have good ideas.
Antagonistic	*"That's a crazy idea...."* This style suggests that the speaker could never come up with a good idea.

Most listeners continually use and fluctuate between these basic characteristics, depending on what is said, who says it, and how it is said. Just as there is no one way to present material, there is no one way to listen effectively. People have and use different listening styles, which are influenced by the way information is presented. A presenter might disseminate content using a very specific and analytical style or use a general (big picture) style. For example, the presentation of a new organizational policy could be presented by covering each department and specific incidence, or presented generally as a worthwhile policy for employees to follow.

How a presenter explains information also affects the listener's interpretation of it. Some people, for instance, take a simple concept and manage to turn it into an abstract brain twister. As a listener, it is imperative that you receive and interpret what is said, gaining a clear interpretation in your own terms. A good listener is proactive; he gets what he wants from a presentation. If the speaker seems open to questions, don't let important ideas go by without clarifying—and verbalizing—your needs. Always keep in mind that the purpose of communication is to create a mutual understanding of the information presented. Words represent acts of reality. Even abstract concepts, such as Einstein's theories, represent conceptual realities; we recognize and think about "black holes" due to the theories Einstein presented.

As indicated earlier, listeners must recognize their own biases and alter their interpretation of what is said. One way to explore your own responses is to imagine yourself in various communication situations and then consider your responses to the listening styles and skills questions listed earlier. How might your responses change according to the situation and speaker?

HOW TO ADDRESS QUESTIONS

When you address your audience's questions, show your interest: make eye contact, nod your head to demonstrate that you accept the speaker and the question. Then:

1. Listen to what is said.
2. Listen to how the question is asked.
3. Pause, allow yourself time to think, then respond.

When addressing questions, it is essential that you listen closely to how the speaker asks questions: the words the speaker uses, and the nonverbal cues that accompany the words. When you respond, be concise. Answer questions in an appropriate, succinct manner that meets the audience's needs as well as those of the asker. If you are confused or you need to have a point clarified before you can respond, interject and ask your own question. Do not let the conversation go on; your partner might assume that there is mutual understanding between you.

When someone asks a question that you are unable to answer readily:

1. Listen attentively without rebuttal; make eye contact and acknowledge the asker.

2. If necessary, ask a question in return. This will give you time to think of an appropriate response. For example:

    — Why do you ask that?
    — That is a very interesting thought. Could you expand on your idea?
    — What do you think the ramifications of that would be?
    — How do you think that could be accomplished?

If you have no answer to a question:

1. Acknowledge that you have no answer.

2. Cite the resources you have available for finding an answer (research, data, personnel, networking system, etc.).

3. Promise the asker that you will follow up on the question and get back to the person.
4. Set a time frame for the follow-up.

Questions should be addressed in the manner in which they were asked. If someone asks a specific question, respond specifically; if someone asks a general question, respond in general terms. Think of the ice cream cone and consider the following example, in which a politician either missed or deflected the question.

Question: Mr. Vice President, do you think we should increase our defense budget by a billion dollars to develop more sophisticated weaponry?

Response: We need a strong America. We need to be proud to be Americans. We need to have a sense of security and a safe place to live and raise our families.

Notice that although the question is quite specific, the response is very general. If you intend to address a question accurately, use the same terms in which it was asked, whether they are specific, general, or a combination of both. You might use the same grammatical structure and vocabulary as that used in the question. Our politician's answer would have been more to the point if he had said, "Yes, we should increase our defense budget," or "No, we should not increase...."

A process called neurolinguistic programming, developed and popularized by R. Bandler and J. Grinder in Frogs Into Princes (1979), can help us better understand the concept of effective communication. If we break down the term "neurolinguistic programming," understanding its central concept is easy: "Neuro" brain function indicates that the five senses are involved, "linguistic" refers to verbal and nonverbal language, and "programming" indicates that communication is organized consciously.

The concept of neurolinguistic programming provides insight into the ways people process information. One important point is that as they speak, people give verbal and nonverbal cues to how they are processing and interpreting information at that moment. The presenter can analyze these cues—classified as visual, auditory, and kinesthetic—to determine the questioner's learning style and formulate a response to the question that employs the same style.

1. "I see what you are saying," "Picture this....," or "Imagine..." are responses to visual cues.

2. "I hear what you are saying," "I'll tell you...," or "Are you attuned to what I said?" are responses to auditory cues.

3. "My gut feeling is....," "Emotionally I agree....," or "I have a sense that..." are responses to kinesthetic cues.

However, sometimes cues are more ambiguous. For example, "I don't understand" cannot be categorized because it is too general and reveals little of the asker's learning style. In such cases, the presenter might first try to clarify the response or offer the audience different cues. Asking, "How do you see this problem?" or "Could you tell us a little more about that?" accomplishes this. Primarily, Bandler and Grinder study of neurolinguistic programming underscores that one must listen carefully to what is

said and then respond with the same sensory concepts. For example, if someone uses visual cues: "I can't picture what you are saying," you might respond visually. Show them something—a slide, a graph, a flip chart—that visually supports what you have said. As you review your point again, use similar language:
— Picture this....
— Can you imagine...?
— In your mind's eye....
— Let me paint the scenario....

Similarly, if someone uses auditory cues :
— I hear what you are saying, but....
— I am not attuned to....
— In response to your question....

Respond with:
— I hear what you are saying....
— I got your message....
— It showed to me that....
— In concert with that....

If someone uses kinesthetic cues:
— I feel that....
— My gut feeling is....
— I am a little gun-shy about....

Respond kinesthetically:
— I am very sensitive to....
— I support what you are saying and....
— I get the feeling that....

In addition to what you should say, be aware of what you should do: stand, sit, walk closer to support your response. Use your intuition. Remember to use other communication aids in conjunction with these verbal responses. Ask yourself what else you can do to help get your message across clearly.

Sharing the style in which the person asks a question helps create mutual understanding. Always listen to what is said and how it is said, then try to respond similarly, in general or specific terms, and follow visual, auditory, or kinesthetic cues.

As a presenter, which role do you assume most often? Why? Do you encourage audience participation? Do you create a "we are in this presentation together" attitude? Why?

BRAINSTORMING AND PROBLEM SOLVING

Brainstorming is gathering ideas from the audience to address a question to which the presenter has no immediate answer, or a question the presenter wants listeners to answer individually. Ideally, this technique involves everyone in the audience; if the group is small enough, each person can give an idea or pass. A presenter can continue this collective sharing until the audience offers no more responses.

Brainstorming is usually effective in addressing a specific problem. Using a chalkboard or other visual aid, the presenter might begin by writing the problem or idea inside a circle. Then the group generates as many general ideas as possible including anything that even vaguely correlates with the problem. Let the ideas flow; nothing should be censured. And write all the ideas down. This technique allows the group to analyze visually a very specific problem or idea in relation to the general ideas that surround it.

Remember the ice cream cone? Lay it on its side; this is one way to visualize problem solving. (See next page.) The ice cream cone model can help you generate and develop new ideas.

Problem Solving Model

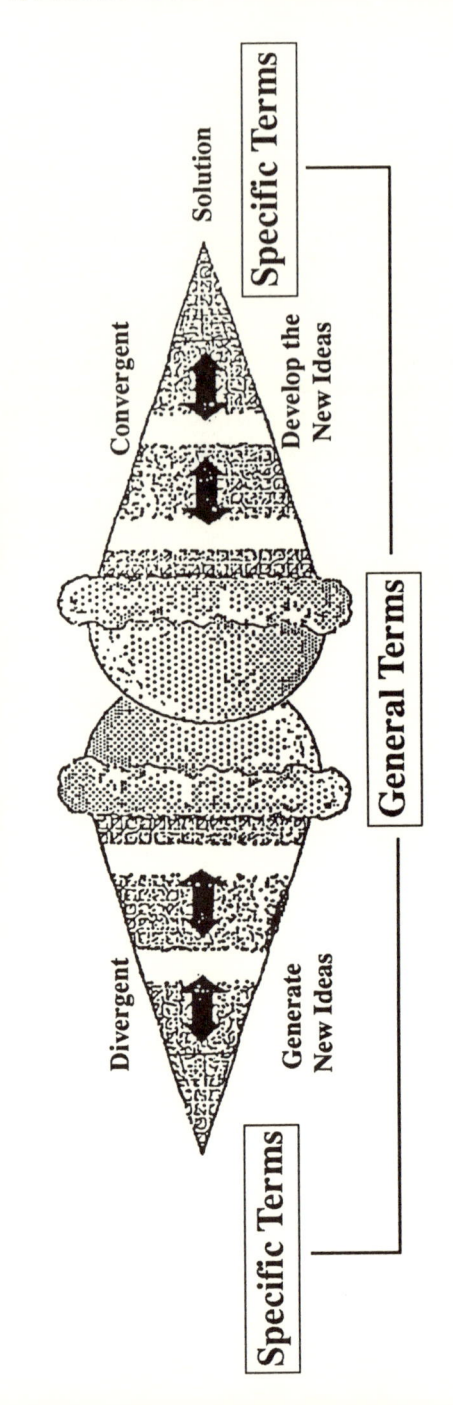

Specific Terms — Solution

Convergent — Develop the New Ideas

General Terms

Divergent — Generate New Ideas

Specific Terms

Following the ice cream cone metaphor, we can compare the general ideas (the ice cream) to the specific ideas (the cone). As the audience, with the presenter's help, defines the problem and chooses a plan to solve it, we reach the tip of the cone. There, a very specific description of the problem and a very specific solution come together. This process can be used any time. And, if you decide that problem solving is necessary to address an audience's needs, this technique offers audience involvement.

Here are six steps for conducting effective brainstorming sessions:

1. Focus on one problem or specific idea. Have a discussion.

2. Write the problem on a visual (paper, chalkboard) and draw a circle around it. Collect responses about the problem. List any idea even remotely related to the problem (general).

3. Write the ideas around the circle. For example:

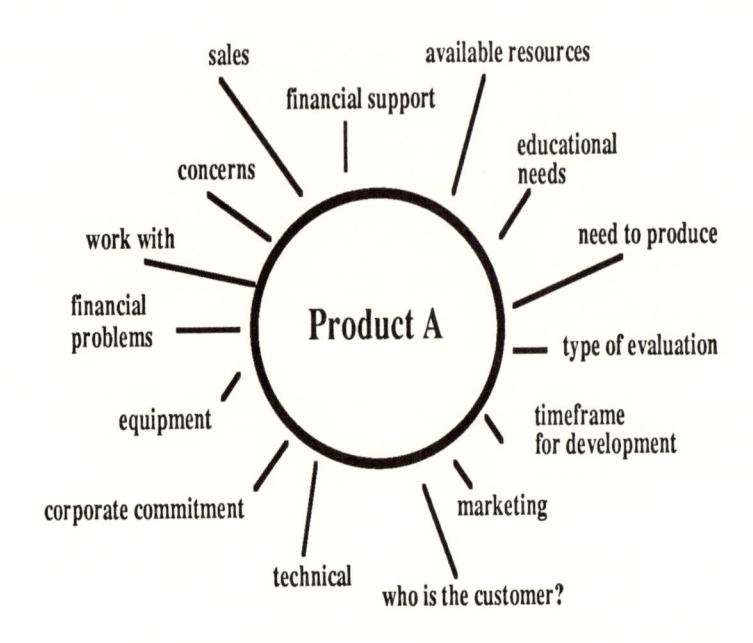

96 *A PRACTICAL GUIDE TO EFFECTIVE PRESENTATION*

```
              sales      available resources
                    financial support
              concerns         educational
                                needs
        work with
                                      need to produce
        financial
        problems      Product A
                                   — type of evaluation
              equipment            timeframe
                                   for development
        corporate commitment   marketing
                        technical
                              who is the customer?
```

4. After the ideas are written, focus on a specific area and list, by priority, the ideas that are pertinent to the discussion. Divide the list into two areas: high priority and low priority. Move from the general to the specific, and try to develop alternatives to the problem. Developing alternatives is a creative way to affect change. For example:

<u>Product A</u>

  (1) Timeframe for development

  (2) Who is the customer?

5. Identify your concerns, then solicit the audience's concerns about the problem. For example:

Product A

    (1)   Timeframe for development

            a) first quarter of first semester

            b) financial support

            c) corporate commitment

6. Now that the problem and its crucial elements are identified, you, as the presenter, can suggest the final steps to solving the problem.

When leading a brainstorming session, an effective presenter acknowledges the audience's input, rather than telling them what they should say or should have said. The presenter listens carefully to all they offer instead of hearing what he/she wants to hear.

Brainstorming Follow-up

Of course, no problem-solving process is complete or successful until someone implements the changes or solutions on which the participants decided. The problem-solving process depends on the 3A's: *Acquire*, *Acknowledge*, and *Act* on information.

Acquire

1. Find the person with the information.
2. Collect unbiased information by asking questions.
3. Clarify what was said by paraphrasing.

Acknowledge

1. Identify problems and state them clearly.
2. Use brainstorming.
3. Have participants discuss possible solutions and summarize.

Act

1. Devise a sequential action plan (specify Step 1, Step 2, etc.).
2. Develop a realistic timeframe for completing the action plan.
3. Create guidelines for reassessing the action plan.

BUILDING AUDIENCE SUPPORT AS A SPEAKER

Earlier we discussed the different roles a presenter might assume to communicate most effectively with the audience. In many ways, the role the presenter chooses determines, to some extent, the complementary role the audience plays. Thus an effective presenter builds a supportive relationship with the audience.

There are many ways to create this relationship. Following are the most important considerations:

1. Speak in a relaxed and friendly voice. Never assume an authoritarian position; the speaker who respects the audience receives respect.

2. Listen to audience responses without appearing judgmental or defensive. If necessary, clarify specific points by questioning in a non-hostile manner.

3. Never attack a listener's character.

4. Encourage audience participation by asking for reactions to what was said, clarification of questions, and explanations of procedures. You also might ask some participants to paraphrase an aspect of the information presented.

5. Never distort facts. If certain information should not be given, withhold it rather than try to disguise it. Distortions always hinder and often destroy a presentation.

6. Focus on the topic the audience expects to hear and use a logical approach to your presentation; small cards with a topic outline or topic sentences serve as aids for an organized, logical approach to speaking.

7. Identify the role that you, as a presenter, want to assume (each role can be effective in the appropriate situation):

   Friend   Arrogant/Hostile
   Experimenter/Inventor   Salesperson
   Authoritarian   Parent
   Representative   Supervisor
   Informer/Compiler of Information   Experienced

8. Identify and use the sensory aids that are most beneficial in presenting your topic.

VISUAL	AURAL	SMELL	TASTE	TOUCH
Appearance	Tapes	Odors from products	Edible product samples	Samples and handouts that show texture, color, size, etc.
Films	Records			
Flip Charts	Speaker/Lecturer			
Handouts				
Graphs				

When choosing sensory aids to support your presentation, choose materials that focus clearly on the presentation topic. After your presentment, as part of your self-critique, analyze the impact of these aids on audience learning. Generally, visual aids are the most effective; it is often by the act of seeing that an audience forms its strongest impressions of the information presented. However, keep in mind that if audience members are examining materials by touching or looking, they are not listening to you. So provide product samples only when appropriate and set aside a specific time for your audience to examine them. Give audience members a chance to inspect your materials and perhaps some time to discuss their reactions among themselves. After they're finished, focus their attention on the next stage of the presentation.

Clearly, the methods a presenter uses to build audience support are most effective when they are an integral part of the presentation. Audience participation, yet another method of building support for your presentation, is a prime example. Earlier in this chapter you saw the audience's participation in the brainstorming/problem-solving process. In this case, the audience clearly becomes an active part of the presentation. But how—and when—does a speaker persuade the audience to take an active part in a presentation that does not focus on problem solving? As suggested earlier, some presenters assume the role of colleague and storyteller: they "volunteer" their personal experiences or perceptions on a topic, then ask members of the audience to contribute their own experiences. In another situation, a presenter might call on a knowledgeable member of the group and ask the person to fill in important details or other information on the subject.

In most cases some audience participation is appropriate. Occasionally, however, an audience is too large to make active participation feasible. Ultimately, as with every other aspect of presentment, the final decision on the amount of audience participation a presenter inspires must rest with understanding of the group and the person's own intuition.

Presentation Environment

As stated earlier, a presentation is influenced by many things: eye contact, hand movements, clothing, facial expressions, time of day, room temperature, lighting, room arrangement, visuals, vocal volume, and so on. Both the presenter and audience react to these environmental influences, so they often markedly affect the presentation as a whole. While some of these influences can be shaped by the presenter, others occur unexpectedly and escape the presenter's "best-laid plans." Regardless of the type of presentation, both presenter and audience should assume active roles to get what they both want from the presentation. The presenter must trust his/her abilities and self-confidence. It also helps to be familiar with as many of these influences as possible. The following notes present some primary considerations:

- Analyze the situation and learn as much about the audience as possible. Communication is situational; ask yourself what is appropriate in this interaction.

- What personality will the audience—and the presentation—have? Should you appear outgoing or quiet? Is your information best presented factually or intuitively? Will your audience expect an analytical, logical speaker or one who is "people-oriented"? What is the purpose of your presentation? Do you wish to appear as a decision-maker or as someone who calls on the audience for a plan of action? A presenter may choose to appear as a "storyteller" by relating experiences and stories; this stance can relax the audience.

- Never caricature the role you take on; if you decide to present yourself as stern and serious, remember that you want to appear professional but not cold and unfeeling. Similarly, while a joke at the right time can relax your audience and build support for your subject, you don't want to appear as a comic nor risk offending anyone.

- Will you alter your speech patterns? Many people use verbal cues, such as "Oh," "Okay," "You know," and "Ah" to punctuate their sentences, to indicate their acceptance of another's ideas, and to signal the end of a conversation. A speaker who depends too heavily on these cues usually sounds monotonous. If these cues are a noticeable part of your speech, note where you tend to use them. To begin sentences? To end them? Sometimes people use cues at the end of sentences to prompt the listener to respond; sometimes the cue only provides a pause—some time to form their next thought. Try replacing cues with silent pauses rather than a "filler" word. Pauses give your audience time to think as well.

  An effective speaker pauses throughout the presentation both to create rhythm and to emphasize important points. Similarly, varying the volume of your voice is a useful way to catch your audience's attention, both in your introduction and at any point you might wish to emphasize.

- Be conscious of the physical distance between you and your listeners. Changing this space can be a tremendous help in directing the audience's attention and establishing a one-on-one communication space with one audience member. Position yourself so you can walk to different areas while speaking. Distance is a technique you can also use in clarifying and supporting questions.

- In some situations the speaker presents while seated with the listeners. In this case, the seat you choose becomes part of your role because it indicates position within the group. Do you want the audience to perceive you as a member of the group (sitting among them) or as their instructor (sitting at the head of the table or room)?

- When your information is best transferred through explanation, or when you stop to explain any point, use visual aids. Diagram your ideas for the listener.

- Be conscious of your time allotment, both for the presentation as a whole and for discussion with the audience. How much time will you spend explaining any one point or answering any one question? Know when to stop. Often the listener's cues will signal you to stop—the person may cross arms, raise one hand, change stance, break eye contact with you, or touch your arm. Be sensitive to these clues.

- If one section of your presentation is particularly detailed or difficult, close it with a brief recap, a sort of mini-summary, to clarify your ideas before you move on to the next point.

- Be aware of your nonverbal responses. What kinds of cues do give with your hands and facial expressions? Be careful not to give mixed messages—to say one thing and yet imply another with your face or gestures.

- Eye contact is the most powerful nonverbal technique, and it can hold an audience's attention. When presenting, try to establish eye contact with members of your group periodically. Look at your audience when addressing questions. Begin by looking at the person who asked the question, then look at others. This will help maintain the audience's interest when addressing questions.
- Be conscious of your body movements. Avoid waving your arms, pointers, or pens; avoid nervous responses such as rolling a pen in your hands or jingling coins in your pocket. Although its good to change position occasionally during your presentment, don't nervously walk around or rock in place. Use the space available to present. When you get to a certain area of the room, stay a while then move. This way you avoid walking around continually.

DEALING WITH HOSTILITY

When giving presentations, occasionally you might encounter a hostile audience member. How should you deal with this situation? Should you ignore the hostility, respond in an equally hostile manner, or even allow the hostile person to have center stage? In truth, none of these will help you to continue your presentation and still hold your audience's attention.

Fortunately, however, there are a number of ways you can maintain control with a hostile group member. First, move a little closer to the person with whom you are interacting—whether it be the hostile audience member or someone else. If you are seated, stand; by changing your stance, you reassert your authority as the presenter. If the person is hostile but presenting useful facts or ideas, go back to the flip chart or board and write them down. This gives the person credit for what is being said and, at the same time, allows the audience to examine the information more objectively, with less of the hostile speaker's verbal and emotional influence.

When the person begins to repeat his ideas, assume that the person has stated at least the most important points. Interject at this point and paraphrase the person's comments to the group. This shows that you are in control while still meeting the hostile person's needs. Decide whether to discuss this point further now or wait for a more appropriate time. Remember, you set the ground rules. At the same time, it's important to consider the position and authority of the disruptive person; your response to a vice president and a first-level manager might differ, at least occasionally. Estimate the risk of addressing or not addressing this issue now. Ask yourself what effect this discussion will have on the rest of your presentation. Consider the politics involved.

If you decide to address the person's concerns during the presentation, guide the discussion and call on other members for their viewpoints. But be careful not to cut the hostile person off too soon. Give the person a chance to vent hostilities while you write pertinent ideas on the board or flip chart. Another technique that often proves effective is to walk over and stand by the hostile person or by any member to whom is person is directing ideas. By moving next to this person, you show support. If conflict between two members erupts as a result of the hostile speaker, stand between the people in conflict. Make eye contact with the speaker and interject your thoughts. Try to refocus the group's attention by addressing the issues raised with facts, not emotions. If it is a long presentation, take a short break after you have regained the group's focus.

The Hostile Audience

So far, we have assumed an audience that is generally receptive to the presenter, allowing for one hostile member. Sometimes a presenter will face a hostile audience. Again, learning as much about your audience as possible when preparing your presentation will help you head off problems. If you are addressing a particularly controversial subject, keep in mind that your audience may be unreceptive to you as well as your subject. As a presenter, be sensitive to your audience's stance. The needs of a hostile audience must be addressed with specific content. When an audience bands together on a specific issue, listen carefully to their ideas and confirm their stance. Never fight emotion with emotion; use verifiable facts.

In addition:

1. Encourage audience participation.

2. Keep pace with audience members by using their style of speech and jargon. Speak on their level.

3. Get a clear understanding of the problem. Listen to what is said and address the issue specifically.

4. If you know the specific problem, state it; offer your information on its background and results.

5. Don't dismiss your audience's concerns or frustrate them further by cutting off their argument or by answering too soon. Negotiate mutual agreement on an issue by listening and then responding.

6. Don't repeat your points too often. Your audience will notice and respond in kind. Your presentation could very easily degenerate into a show of wills.

7. Stay with the topic until your expectations are met. Control the discussion by asking questions, listening to their responses, and responding to them.

8. Recap the discussion by addressing the major issues verbally and, if possible, visually using a flip chart or overhead.

9. If possible, take a five-minute break.

Look for support within your audience and stick to your information. However, if you have no answer to a question, admit it.

The Disrupter

As a presenter, you may have to distinguish between a hostile audience member with valid concerns and someone who disrupts your presentation merely to manipulate the audience. Because disruptive group members can hinder the communication flow between you and the rest of your audience, you should intervene quickly. A common form of disruptive behavior is people talking among themselves instead of listening to the speaker. This form of disruption is usually easy to handle. Ask the disruptive people if they have a question, thereby calling attention to them. Then wait a few seconds; the audience will look at them. Of course there is a risk in doing this, but it is a surefire way to get the attention of the people talking. Remember: If people are talking, they are not listening.

As a presenter, you must have the confidence and presence of mind to offer group members your facilitation and leadership in an open, honest, trusting, and respectful manner. This will be of great benefit both to the group and you.

PRESENTING BAD NEWS

Bad news is part of doing business, and someday you may be called upon to bear bad tidings. Whether it's a workforce reduction, the loss of an account, or delays in manufacturing, when relating bad news it is important to be specific and organized. Support the audience. If there is resistance, honor it using responses like, "I understand, but . . ." as opposed to "That is ridiculous . . . ."

When giving bad news, never begin with, "I have bad news." Instead, make a more neutral statement, "I have the information on . . ." "I have an update for you on . . ." "I've been following the situation and . . ." "An update on your account/order indicates . . ." or "I am here to discuss . . . ." If you begin by saying, "I have bad (or good) news, the audience will react emotionally rather than listen objectively.

Presenting bad news is a no-win situation, and your best stance will be one that neither minimizes the issues nor criticizes those involved. Be supportive and professional in presenting the information. Follow your presentation design, and move quickly to the specific details. In addition:

1. Be proactive. When you learn of the bad news, create a strategy to deliver it promptly. If your audience gets the information elsewhere, their trust in you will be jeopardized. Remember to use your techniques for dealing with a hostile audience.

2. Present the facts. Don't complain about the organization or anyone involved. The effects of knocking the organization are short-term and can come back to haunt you.

3. Create a mutual understanding. If possible, discuss business alternatives or follow-up action.

4. Be as positive as possible; be confident and even enthusiastic, to a point. Honor any resistance your audience expresses. Respond with statements such as, "I understand why you would be upset, but these are the facts . . . ." Remain calm and objective. Use notes to support what you say. Visuals are helpful.

5. Remind the audience of other successes. Try to win small concessions. Rather than try to solve the larger issue, break it into smaller fragments or phases. State the problem specifically and clearly: "I want to discuss with you changes in . . . the costs of . . . the delivery date . . . the quality of . . . the specs . . . ." Hedging on the issue or withholding information your audience clearly wants will appear uncooperative and irresponsible.

6. Raise the issue of trust in you and the group you represent, using statements like, "We are doing our best . . . ." Give specific reasons for the problem and express your support for the audience and their concerns: "We want to work with you . . . ," "We understand you are angry or disappointed . . . ," or "Let's work out what we can do . . . ." Stay with your audience verbally. Address their questions and avoid the attacking style of communication.

7. Follow up. This is a key to creating credibility and trust. Establish a convenient time to present new facts or have further discussion. Be cautious of what you put in writing.

8. Be reassuring. If your contact is face-to-face, make eye contact; if it is by phone, paraphrase and summarize.

9. Remember to present yourself and the organization in a professional manner. How you present yourself and the facts will influence the audience's response and outcome.

10. Summarize: State your conclusions, outcomes, results, and follow-up action. This final stage can be very important to your audience's impression of you.

GRAPHICS

The purpose of graphics is to create an analysis or comparison of content that would otherwise take a great deal of verbal description. A graphic should stand on its own, having its own title, data format, explanation key, and so on. It should be colorful and easily comprehended. A graphic should read like a book. Therefore, writing words vertically (for instance, along the vertical axis of a graph) is not always effective. In choosing a graphic to present your data, remember that comprehension and application of data are your primary considerations.

Graphics play an important role in planning a presentation. They act as support for your information and give the audience options in gaining an understanding. Letting the audience analyze a graphic can create many different approaches to presenting both specific and general information. Any and all graphics can be used in a general or specific context, depending on the level of verbal explanation the audience expects and what the presenter wants to accomplish. There is one general principle for graphics: Keep them simple. Complex images and too much data in a graphic neither clarify your message nor help the audience gain a better understanding. When choosing or designing your graphics, use blues, greens, and other vibrant colors that remain visible with the lights out. Be careful when you use the color red: it can suggest an alarm or barrier.

Another important consideration in designing your presentation is selecting and preparing materials. Each form—handouts, visuals, graphics, etc.—requires different preparation. A handout should not be copied "as is" and used as an overhead visual, nor should a visual be substituted for prepared text. It is important to decide what materials you will use for what purposes and to have all materials well-planned and prepared ahead of time.

When using a graph, present the audience with a brief explanation or mental assignment. For example, ask the audience how to apply the graph, state the problem it represents, and the function it serves.

Many presenters copy their overhead visuals and distribute them as handouts. Before you follow this practice, stop and reflect on exactly what you'd like to accomplish with your graphics. Prepared text should be titled and formatted to show clear and precise thought. Many times, this involves a setup very different from a visual format. Usually the bullet format is an effective structure for overhead visuals. (Figure 1). This format presents concepts in phrases instead of sentences or paragraph form, assuming that your audience needs only a brief visual reinforcement of your verbal presentment. Using these visuals as handouts may be inappropriate because they merely repeat information out of context. Similarly, an effective handout usually offers too much data to function as an effective visual.

Figure 1
Bullet Format

Suggestion: When making a comparison between concepts, place them across from each other rather than underneath.

- concept 1   • concept A
- concept 2   • concept B
- concept 3   • concept C
- concept 4   • concept D

Consider this example as a bullet format, suitable for an overhead visual.

Effective Presentation

- Know why you are presenting.
- Know the content.
- Know the expected results.
- Know the time restrictions.

The purpose of the bullet (•) is to mark a point without indicating the hierarchy inherent in numbers or alphabetical order. The presenter suggests a pattern or order of importance with an explanation of the visual. A text handout, on the other hand, must guide the reader through the material with little help from the presenter.

At this point, stop again and consider the questions that guide your preparation for presentment:

Questions in Designing a Presentation

1. Why am I speaking?
2. What do I want to accomplish?
3. Why should the audience listen to me?
4. With whom am I speaking?
5. How long should I speak?
6. Is this presentation to be persuasive or informative?
7. Does this presentation have to agree with, precede, or follow another presentation?
8. How should I present my material?

These questions can be helpful in designing the following graphics:

Quadrant Graphic

This graphic should be used to identify different products/characteristics on a quality basis.

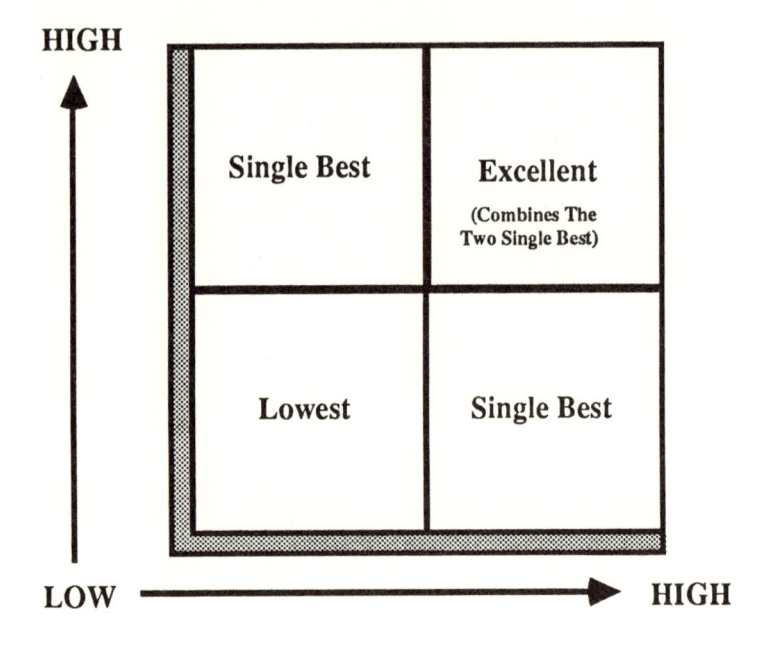

HIGH ↑	Single Best	Excellent (Combines The Two Single Best)
	Lowest	Single Best
LOW →		**HIGH**

Line Graphic

This graphic should be used to show comparisons, individual growth analysis, or other individual factors.

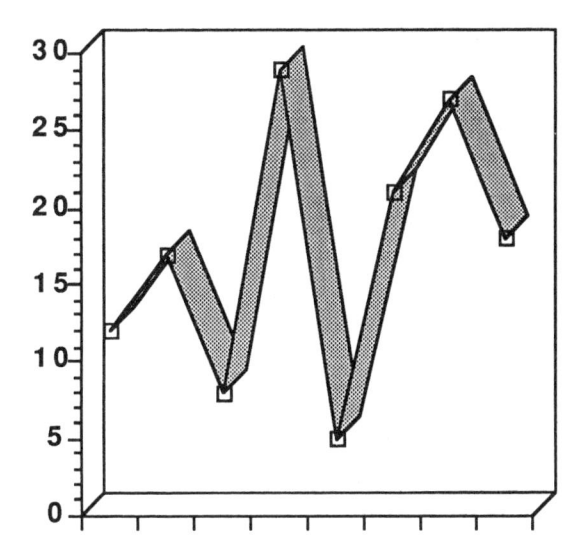

Pie Graphic

This graphic should be used to identify individual ideas within the total concept.

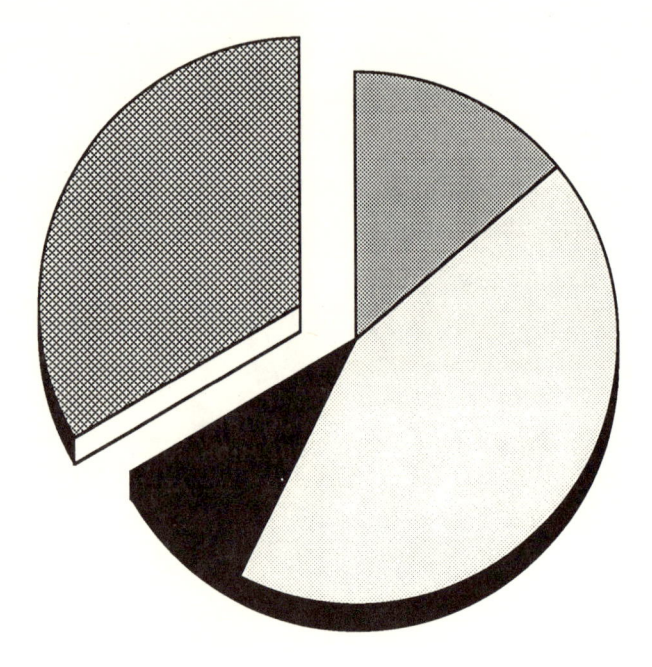

Bar Graphic

This graphic should be used to identify individual comparisons.

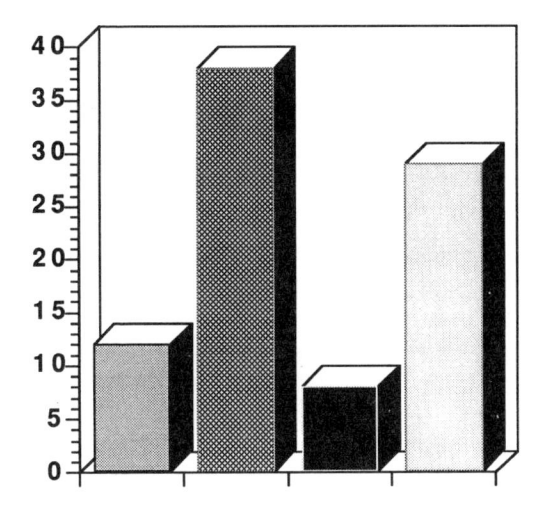

PRACTICAL SUGGESTIONS FOR USING VISUAL AIDS

When you first present a visual, ask the audience to read it to themselves. Do not begin to talk or read the visual aloud. Watch the audience. They will look at you after they've finished reading and are ready for additional information. This is your signal to begin speaking.

Evaluate your own graphics:

1. Does the graphic represent what I would otherwise explain?

2. Is the graphic colorful and easy to read?

3. Can the graphic stand alone without explanation? (A graphic must represent a complete concept independent of an oral description.)

Flip Charts

1. You can use flip charts or a transparency as an icebreaker prior to speaking. For example, the first page might read: Good morning. Welcome to the Presentation. Your name.

2. You can use flip charts to display an outline of the presentation. This same visual also can serve as the basis of your summary.

3. You can use flip charts as a visual divider, along with transparencies, separating sections that present new or different information. This helps the audience follow a change of topic. One or two phrases on each page is enough.

4. You can use flip charts to record the audience's responses to important questions. The response pages can be placed on the wall for visual reference. This also will help you remember to address questions later in the presentation.

5. You can prepare flip chart pages before the presentation and tape them to the wall for visual reference of statements or definitions.

6. Use colored markers to create visual interest and emphasize a particular word or concept. Make the pages colorful.

7. When using a flip chart, write notes lightly in pencil next to what you have written with markers. Your penciled notes will be visible only to you. The audience's eyes are drawn to the bright ink colors and you have a created support system for yourself.

8. Stand to the side of the flip chart and use your hand or a pointer, if needed, to address a specific topic written on the chart. Anchoring yourself to the flip chart will prevent you from walking around excessively.

9. Today many abbreviations and acronyms have found their way into the business world. Many presenters repeat an acronym which has another meaning. For small groups, a good use of a flip

chart would be to write out the entire word(s), with the abbreviation or acronym in parentheses. Put the flip chart page on a wall prior to the presentation. Refer to it in the overview. By leaving it on the wall, the audience can refer to the abbreviations or acronyms as needed.

10. For large groups of fifty or more (depending on the room), a flip chart may be difficult to read. As a backup, distribute a handout explaining any abbreviations or acronyms prior to the presentation, or show a visual (overhead or slide) that notes abbreviations and acronyms.

Overhead Transparencies

1. Clear transparencies can be produced on most photocopiers. Use colored pen(s) for emphasis or highlighting.

2. Always frame (mount) the transparency or purchase 3M Transparencies® that have a painted white border. Use the frame as a visual aid for yourself by writing reference notes on it. The frame also provides a visual border, and it gives your work a professional look.

3. Use an extended pointer, standing to the side of the screen and pressing it against the screen to avoid any distracting movement. Use a retracted pointer, placing it on the transparency next to the topic you are addressing.

4. If possible, have transparencies you use often produced professionally. Computerized transparencies are usually the most effective due to their professional look. Use a black background with various highlight colors.

5. A trick in using the overhead project is to tape a square piece of paper over the top mirror. This allows you to turn the projector on and off silently without wasting time on cords or cooling fans.

6. Never put too much information on a transparency. Use large print and open spacing.

7. When comparing information, list your points across from each other, instead of stacking them. This method is very effective, for instance, when you're offering an audience alternatives to a problem.

8. Every transparency should be self-explanatory and have a title.

9. Use the top two-thirds of the screen for presenting.

10. Using the overhead projector while seated is an effective way to present. It allows you to look at your audience and read off of the projector without blocking their view of the visual.

Slides

1. View all slides prior to the presentation. Compare their appearance with the lights on and off to note the visual effect. Use colors that project and blend well.
2. Avoid slides with too much information.
3. Choose slides that are visually interesting.
4. Every slide should be self-explanatory and have a title.
5. Tighten the top of the slide carousel to ensure the best projection and to prevent the slides from falling out. If a slide gets stuck, use a paper clip to free it. Bend it into an "L" shape, reach down and pull up on the slide until it falls into place. Try to remain calm if this happens; it's a common problem.
6. Check all equipment before you present.
7. Use the top two-thirds of the screen for presenting.

Use color in all your visuals. Use red for titles or to emphasize a word or concept. Use blue, green, and darker colors for general information. Avoid light colors such as yellows and pinks; they have little visual impact.

Chalkboard

1. You can use a chalkboard to outline or highlight a presentation.
2. If available, use colored chalk and write neatly and large enough to be read easily.
3. Stand to the side and use a pointer to refer to particular topics within the outline. Underline key words.

Microphone

1. When using a lavaliere microphone, position it where your second button on a shirt or blouse would be.
2. When using a stationary microphone, do not stand too close to the microphone or the audience will hear every breath you take.

Presentation Kit

Effective presenters come prepared to meet the needs created by various venues and audiences. To meet this challenge, bringing a presentation kit to every presentation is a must The kit contains these items:

- Large paper clips (a pre-bent clip in the shape of an "L" for jammed slides is helpful)
- Masking tape to post flip chart pages and to make repairs
- Scissors

- Rubber bands
- Marking pens
- Overhead transparencies and pens
- Pens and pencils with erasers
- Stick pins to post flip chart pages on felt or carpeted walls
- Pointer that extends approximately two feet
- Plug adapter—3 to 2 prong
- Stapler and staple remover
- Stopwatch
- Calculator

If you use slides, carry a small extension cord in the carousel box.

EMPHASIZING KEY CONCEPTS IN CONJUNCTION WITH A VISUAL

Using a Pointer

1. If you are not using the pointer, put it in your pocket or put it down.

2. Generally, a pointer is used to indicate specific information on a visual. Sometimes a closed pointer can be used on a clear transparency to emphasize an idea.

3. Put the pointer in the hand closest to the visual. If you are to the right of the visual, use your right hand and vice-versa. Be careful not to use your right hand when presenting on the left side of the visual. This will force you to face the visual. As a result, you will lose eye contact with the audience and, instead, talk to the visual.
4. When using a pointer, place it to the side of the information you want the audience to note. Push the pointer against the screen slightly. This will prevent you from shaking the pointer in mid-air.
5. Remember that a pointer is a tool, not a toy, a weapon, or an eradicator of stress.
6. Alternatives to a pointer:

   — Highlight information in bright colors. If you want a concept to really stand out, circle it in red.

   — Use a flashlight arrow to emphasize information. (For best results, this should be used only in darkened rooms.)

   — Use the building technique: show one concept in a visual, then build upon it by revealing the next concept. Instead of showing the entire visual and discussing all the concepts, you build upon the concept. This works well, for example, when discussing a manufacturing process or flow chart.

— Use different rates and patterns of speech to emphasize key concepts on a visual. For example: State the concept loudly and slowly, then pause two to three seconds.

Keep in mind that your purpose is to draw the audience's attention to a particular concept on a visual, which is meant to reinforce and emphasize it. Remember to take your time when presenting key points.

SETTING UP THE ROOM

Usually, you will have little information on how the presentation room will be arranged. However, when you do, take these ideas into consideration:

1. Set up the room so you can move around and everyone can still see you. Don't stand at a lectern. Let the audience see you. Remember that you act as a moving visual.

2. Set up the room so you can move closer to any participant you address individually. This helps build rapport.

3. If possible, open the drapes to provide natural lighting, which can also make the room appear larger.

Room Design

It is important to use the entire room and all available resources. Move to both sides of the room to break the distance and barriers of space. Moving closer to people increases concentration on the subject, both yours and theirs. If you are having a two-way discussion, move closer to the person involved.

When showing a visual, move to the outside of the audience, possibly to the middle of the room. This will increase your volume and bring you closer to the people in the back. Remember that people in the front have a better rapport with the speaker simply because they are closer. Break the distance, and get to the people in the back of the room.

The "U" shape and Chevron room designs allow participants to have eye contact with each other and permit the presenter to move closer to the audience.

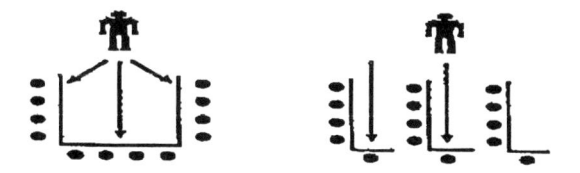

U Shape

Chevron

Note: try to avoid the classroom design. Participants in the back of the room have less speaker interaction and cannot see the other participants.

Group Dynamics

Your movements can change the group dynamics. Sit for a relaxed presentation; stand for a formal or authoritarian presentation. How do you want to be perceived? What tone do you want to set? For example if you are a supervisor or middle-manager presenting to executives, stand to show authority and self-confidence. If you are presenting in a round table discussion, remain seated to be perceived as a member of the group. Question yourself as to how you want to be perceived.

SUMMARY

Become aware of your individual style of presentment. It is important that you continually assess and reassess the uniqueness and purpose behind your presenting. This assessment will enable you to develop a presentment style that is comfortable to you and engages the audience. Remember that graphics and room setup help to establish the climate of the presentation and, so, are essential to its effectiveness.

Personal Checklist for Presenting

This checklist will help you in the planning and presentation stages. You might find it helpful to write notes to yourself about these ideas.

1. Be enthusiastic. Never let the audience feel you have something better to do.

2. Try to arrive at the presentation room early. Greet people, introduce yourself. If you have a nametag, put it on your right side; it allows people to see your name when you shake hands.

3. Breathe slowly and deeply from your diaphragm. Try not to sound out of breath.

4. Be aware of your facial expressions. Saying, "I'm glad to be here" with a frown on your face sends the audience the wrong message.

5. Make eye contact with the audience. You can pick up energy from the audience and also signs of confusion. Do not overreact to your audience, but do reach to them.

6. Dress according to audience expectations and the situation.

7. Never fondle pens, chalk, or pointers. Keep one hand down (in a side pocket) and the other waist high for movement and emphasis. Be careful not to gesture too often. If you have no pockets or you don't want to keep your hands in them, put one hand to your side (usually the one you use least), and pinch some material between your thumb and index finger.

8. Don't walk around. If you do move around the room, arrive and visit. Touch your leg or hand to a chair, table, flip chart—this will help curb the urge to nervously walk around.

9. Try not to show nervousness. No one but you knows what you are going to say next.

10. Be aware of your posture. Show confidence by standing erect.

11. Define the role you are assuming for this presentation (informer/compiler of information, experimenter/ inventor, parent, friend, authoritarian, salesperson, representative, supervisor-to-subordinate).

12. Keep in mind that the presentation begins before you speak and continues after you leave. The presentation begins when you accept to present and continues as long as people think about what you presented and how you presented it.

CHAPTER 6

PRESENTING IN A BUSINESS MEETING

"High on the diagnostic checklist of corporate health is communication. The ease with which information flows downward, upward, and horizontally is often a major internal indicator of organizational effectiveness; who listens to whom may reveal the real as opposed to the apparent authority structure in a firm; and the proportion of people who consistently fail to get the message is frequently taken as a statistical baseline for predicting the efficiency with which plans will be translated into action."

(Hall, 1988, p. 216)

In the business environment, time is at a premium; however, time is continually lost in meetings, an area crucial to the success of any business. It's essential that meetings be productive and meet business objectives efficiently. Presentation lies at the heart of successful business meetings, and yet too often time is wasted by mini-presentations that run past time allotments and repeat material that has already been presented. This chapter examines the steps necessary to conduct effective business meetings, ones that include quality presentations that fulfill the expectations and objectives of each participant.

SUGGESTIONS FOR BUSINESS MEETING PRESENTATIONS

When giving a presentation, it is best to arrive well before the audience. This allows you time to check equipment and room setup. Then, when the audience begins to arrive, you are relaxed and ready to greet them. Many presenters use lecterns, but keep in mind that a lectern acts as a barrier and creates distance between you and the audience.

Consider the following points relative to business presentations:

1. These presentations should first be given "in-house" to the business teams most involved in and affected by the content.

    a. This shares technical knowledge and results in coordinated information to the customer.

    b. It gives the presenters a chance to practice their skills. This should be done twice a year.

2. Show the company logo, title of presentation, and your name on the screen or flip chart as the audience walks in. This sets the tone and serves as a good visual.
3. The introduction is crucial. Know it well, be confident, and let the audience know you are knowledgeable and will share information and ideas.
4. Emphasize how your corporation "connects" to the customer in terms of research, application, and development. State how this connection benefits the customer.
5. Also present new or future research and development. Tell the audience why your corporation is a leader in the field.
6. The diversity of your corporation is important if you can present a common theme or show how divisions overlap. For example: _____is a leader in these areas. . ." or "Researchers in another division have developed . . . ."
7. Present hard data about your corporation. No presenter should say, "We are the best" without providing supporting data. Consider the following lead-ins to supporting data:

   "Our corporation stands for quality because of our research, development, manufacturing, and technical services."

   "Our corporation stands for quality: manufacturing is the first step to quality, technical service is the second step."

   "Our corporate representatives will work with you every step of the way."

"Our corporate representatives are your technical partners and, like you, have a commitment to excellence."

"Our corporation is the one to call for service."

LEADING A BUSINESS MEETING

A business meeting must be more than a group of people coming together to express general opinions about the business climate; it must have a focused direction and fulfill specific business expectations. An effective meeting can and should address both immediate and long-term issues. By structuring the combined energies and personalities brought together in business meetings, both the organization and individual participants benefit.

A business meeting has three basic functions:

1. To identify and specifically address business issues in a specified timeframe.
2. To create a forum in which viewpoints are exchanged constructively and safely while addressing the identified business issues.
3. To establish a plan of action, short- or long-term, which specifies necessary action (i.e., the delegation of responsibility to individuals) or follow-up discussion at another meeting. Meetings potentially offer a method for a department or division to develop its influence in the organization.

The meeting leader, or facilitator, is responsible for keeping the meeting focused, promoting discussion, and delegating follow-up action. More specifically, the facilitator is responsible for:

- identifying appropriate business issues or concerns or, in other words, preparing an agenda;
- writing and distributing a premeeting memo specifying that agenda;
- setting a specific amount of time in which to hold the meeting and adhering to the agenda items within the allotted timeframe;
- procuring a room and necessary equipment;
- notifying members of the meeting time and place;
- controlling the flow of the meeting and ensuring that discussion is focused on agenda items;
- giving an overview of what is to be accomplished, guiding the discussion of specific issues, summarizing the meeting, adjourning the meeting, and distributing follow-up information.

The facilitator's chief responsibility is to control the energy and focus of the meeting. However, this doesn't mean the facilitator is the only one who should speak; rather, it suggests that the facilitator should strive to ensure that all business issues or concerns are addressed properly.

An effective facilitator understands the communication dynamics in a meeting and uses them. For example, conflict is not necessarily damaging to meetings. An open, honest exchange of ideas—even though they differ—can often generate creative solutions. The facilitator should identify controversial issues by paraphrasing them and drawing all members into a productive sharing of ideas. By doing this, the facilitator maintains the members' interest, focuses the meeting, and allows everyone the opportunity to express their point of view. Acknowledging disagreement among meeting members can be a catalyst for creating the invigorating environment required of a thought-provoking, successful business meeting. Rather than avoiding conflict, the effective facilitator uses it.

The key to an effective business meeting is beginning with a solid plan. A good facilitator organizes an agenda, speakers, and length of discussion ahead of time to ensure that the group discusses crucial issues and reaches its meeting goals. Likewise, a good plan establishes the appropriate length of time for a meeting. The meeting must be long enough to meet its objectives yet still hold the interest of each member. "Marathon" should not be a synonym for "business meeting."

In addition, the actual starting time of a meeting, to some extent, determines its potential success. Never make the starting time of a meeting on the hour or half-hour. Most business meetings begin at those times because people arrange their schedules by the hour or half-hour. They make phone calls on the hour, break on the hour, meet on the hour, and so on. Because of this programming, people often come five or ten minutes late to meetings that are scheduled on the hour or half-hour. Start the meeting 15 or 20 minutes after or before the hour. Make the meeting room available at least 15 minutes before the scheduled meeting time. Serve coffee, tea, and soft drinks and then begin the meeting on time. This creates a relaxed but organized business atmosphere and allows time for small discussions prior to the meeting.

Hints on Improving Meeting Effectiveness

1. Prepare a premeeting memo that lists the people invited to attend, issues to be discussed, and time schedule.
2. Prepare a meeting agenda; make extra copies.
3. Prior to the meeting, check to ensure that all audiovisual equipment to be used is working correctly.
4. Stand when you begin the meeting. For an informal discussion, sit down after the meeting is called to order. Seat yourself strategically, either at the end or directly in the middle of the conference table.
5. Allow top management the flexibility to address their specific issues and leave.
6. Anticipate group interaction.
7. As a facilitator, provide the service of collecting the group's thoughts.
8. When no new viewpoints on a topic are shared, or when old viewpoints are repeated, interject and move the meeting on to the next stage. Repetition leads to boring meetings.
9. Table issues that cannot be resolved and assign follow-up action for a later meeting.

10. Control the meeting to stay within established time constraints. Never let a disruptive participant sideline the organization of the meeting.
11. Follow up a business meeting by distributing information to all appropriate employees.

As leader (facilitator) of a business meeting, you must have the confidence and ability to control the meeting's structure and flow. The meeting is no time to renew old acquaintances or talk about unrelated subjects; it is a time to discuss pertinent business issues. A business meeting benefits participants because it informs them of significant issues and it utilizes their combined energies to raise relevant, thought-provoking questions. Raising the right questions about a specific issue results in thoughtful discussion and effective follow-up action.

Follow-up action includes distributing the meeting minutes to the appropriate executives, managers, professionals, and support staff. Since the purpose of a business meeting, like any presentation, is to collect, share, and disseminate information, all appropriate employees should be informed of meeting results. In this way, the action agreed to in the meeting can be firmly established.

Follow-up is essential in evaluating the overall effectiveness of the meeting. A meeting begins with preparation and planning; it concludes when the facilitator evaluates the interactions that occurred during the meeting, and the effectiveness of the follow-up action.

Building Rapport

1. The meeting actually begins when you greet members as they enter the room. This is when you begin to shape and stimulate a professional atmosphere in which members can feel both comfortable and serious about achieving group objectives. If this is the first meeting of this group, have the members introduce themselves. If the group has already met, introduce only the new members. Remember that the instant a person enters the room, you are responsible for establishing the climate of the meeting. After everyone is seated, choose a seat either at the head of the table or the middle, depending on how you want to be perceived. As noted previously, sitting at the middle of the table implies that you want to be viewed as an equal member in the meeting. Sitting at the head of the table implies that you are the leader and are to provide direction.

2. Be "other" directed. Think about the group's interests; be sensitive to their needs and present the agenda items at a pace and level of comprehension suitable to all participants.

3. Use your voice and visuals to create interest. Don't speak in a monotone; concentrate on vocal inflection as a means of creating excitement. Varying your rate of speech can subtly attract the listeners' attention and make your presentation more interesting. Move around the room and use body movements and eye contact to create an energetic and lively atmosphere. This, in turn, will enhance listener

interest and improve your communication with the group.

4. Know the agenda and stick to it. Be aware of any new information regarding agenda items. Don't allow a disruptive meeting member to cause you to stray from the agenda. Interject strongly, if necessary, to keep the meeting flowing.

5. Don't let the meeting continue past the timeframe stated in the premeeting agenda memo.

Process Vs. Content

A meeting should include substantive topics interesting enough to motivate group discussion. However, regardless of actual content matter, the way a group processes that content determines the outcome of the meeting. Further, the discussion and interaction that take place during the meeting may also determine its results.

As meeting leader, you should create a safe environment that not only controls and stimulates the open sharing of ideas among members, but also takes into consideration group needs and agenda topics. You can begin fostering a safe environment by building trust and removing doubts among group members. This challenges your ability to consider group needs while maintaining control of the meeting. Establish, as specifically as possible, your expectations of the meeting and the actions you expect to result from it. Interject enough to control discussion; however, never stifle the creative process. A safe environment encourages open, honest, and respectful communication. Successful communication requires that every member feel that they are a part of the meeting and capable of making significant contributions to the discussion. You can encourage positive participation by identifying roles for all active members, even if they only plan to attend one meeting. Help the members feel included in the meeting by encouraging them to share their information and ideas. Keep in mind that you are there to help the group reach its goals. To do so, you must take advantage of group interaction energies. As meeting leader or facilitator, you must ensure that information and ideas are processed in a manner that is safe and productive for every participant.

Positive Interaction

The purpose of a business meeting is to reach a positive and productive outcome. You can and should add your own thoughts to the discussion, supporting others' ideas and giving corrective feedback by developing alternatives or suggestions for change. To say a meeting has a "positive outcome" does not mean that the actions or discussions were all supportive, nor does it preclude corrective statements. To the contrary: Corrective discussions in a meeting often contribute to its "positive outcome." As part of the meeting process, an effective leader facilitates both supportive and corrective discussion, because both styles represent a positive, open sharing of ideas. The words "negative meeting" or "negative statements" are irrelevant. If a meeting results in supportive or corrective discussions that require follow-up action, that meeting is productive.

Summary

Ultimately it's up to you, the meeting leader, to organize the structure and process of the meeting and shape the group's energy and interaction. Keep in mind that, like the formal presentation, the process of a meeting is just as important as the content discussed. To create a stimulating business environment capable of fulfilling meeting objectives, encourage each member to share a point of view with the group. Create a safe environment, where members feel confident that they will be heard and acknowledged; stimulate discussion (both supportive and corrective) that leads to follow-up action. Stick to the agenda and end the meeting within the given time constraints. These methods go far toward creating the ideal meeting structure and atmosphere. Satisfying group needs will help you, in turn, satisfy your own needs as meeting leader or facilitator.

TIME MANAGEMENT IN MEETINGS

Effective time management is crucial to the success of a business meeting. A facilitator manages time by adhering to a well-planned agenda, using problem-solving techniques that consider changing environments and available resources, and motivating all members to focus their energies on the main priorities of the meeting. Because you are in charge of the meeting, you are responsible for meeting time constraints.

Consider the following tools and techniques for conducting efficient meetings:

1. Develop an action plan that coincides with the agenda. To do this, you must consider the participants, speakers, topics, and meeting situation. For example, imagine you have invited a speaker to address budget issues, but to adhere to the meeting agenda, you know his talk must be kept to ten minutes. The best way to assure that you will keep to a schedule is to interject when the speaker has talked for eight or nine minutes and then ask him to summarize.
2. Take time to reflect on what should be accomplished in the meeting; write your thoughts.
3. Focus your energies on completing items noted in the action plan and controlling and stimulating meeting interactions.
4. Accomplish follow-up responsibilities within an established timeframe.
5. Practice problem-solving techniques that use time efficiently. Members should have a clear understanding of their roles and relation to the meeting's goals in the anticipated timeframe.
6. Analyze your greatest time problems (for instance, an outspoken member) and plan accordingly. Clearly establish the ground rules for discussion time in the meeting.

OVERCOMING ROUTINE OBSTACLES

Interruptions/Phone Calls

A phone call in the middle of a meeting will distract members and destroy the flow of the discussion. Arrange in advance to hold all incoming calls for meeting members. Unexpected interruptions should not be tolerated, and no one should be called out of the meeting unless it is an emergency.

Disrupters

This is a member who disrupts the meeting process by introducing topics not on the agenda or repeats ideas or information unnecessarily. The leader should control the meeting and the disrupter by methods such as standing, interjecting, and refocusing the meeting to agenda items.

Organizational Problems

Organizational problems result from poor planning and preparation, and failure to assign roles to each member. Clearly identify the role or function of every participant, even if the member is attending only one meeting. Consider every member a resource of unique creative input; organize the meeting so that this resource will be tapped to generate new ideas.

Poor Interaction

Poor group interaction is often a sign of lack of interest or trust among members. If this is the case, stop all interaction and address issues of interest or trust. You might also discuss ways the group might work together more effectively and how the group's collective input affects the processing of meeting content. Encourage members to share their points of view and let the group build its own rapport from within.

Maturity Level of the Group

Like individuals, group personalities change and mature with time. During the first meeting, members will be polite and more formal. Eventually, as members become better acquainted, personality differences will emerge. Subsequent meetings will then lead to the development of small cliques and support networks within the group, which tend to form around participants with more forceful characteristics; these leaders will develop into the influencers and decision-makers of the group.

You can use the group's maturity level to help accomplish meeting objectives. As you gain a better understanding of the individuals in the meeting, you can assign appropriate tasks, challenge different members to work together, recognize every member's contribution, and follow up on each member's role and responsibilities. Every group has its particular strengths and weaknesses, its own likes and dislikes. Based on the topic and climate of each meeting, you should learn to control the group's interest and maturity level.

Stress

Though feeling "stressed out" is a common experience, the cause of stress varies with every individual. Groups, like individuals, experience stress and undergo serious reactions to pressure and tension. Possible causes of stress include time constraints, interruptions, personality conflicts, and the feeling of having to be two places at once. It's often a good idea to discuss causes of stress during the meeting, especially if stress is evident in the group.

Unclear Expectations

Group expectations must be clearly established, otherwise group energy and interaction will lack focus. One way to communicate meeting objectives effectively is to discuss possible agenda topics with group members prior to the meeting. This helps you create an action plan that allows both you and the group to measure how well your collective meeting expectations are met. The best way to accomplish a collective goal is to define each member's expectations and measure group progress in light of them.

DESIGNING A WRITTEN PRESENTATION

A good business writer must explain thoughts and intentions clearly. Here are some tips for writing effectively:

1. Outline your presentation. Include topic sentences followed by a clear explanation of

their meaning. Shape the content of your document like a conversation, moving from general to specific thoughts. Paraphrase or refer to other documents to support and organize your thoughts.
2. Establish clear priorities in your document and. make sure you have used a logical, organized format to state your meaning. Underline words or sentences to emphasize important thoughts.
3. Use simple, everyday language. No one is impressed by writing they cannot understand. When presenting information, make sure it is written logically and, coherently.
4. It is essential that every document be free of grammatical and spelling errors. If possible, ask a colleague to proofread your presentation. However, always remember that you are responsible for the accuracy of your documents.

Hints on Presenting Your Thoughts in Writing

1. Write your ideas as clearly and simply as possible. To check the flow and clarity of your writing, read the finished document aloud, or ask someone else to proofread it.
2. Never use jargon that your reader might not understand. (Jargon refers to specialized words that relate to a specific job responsibility or type of work). For example, computer operators use jargon such as "upscale" and "wysiwyg."

3. Keep a dictionary and thesaurus close by to help you spell correctly, define words, and find synonyms.

4. Every complete sentence must have a verb (action/word) and subject. A sentence fragment expresses an incomplete thought and may confuse your reader (e.g., The new facility, with its large storage area).

5. The subject and verb of each sentence must agree. For example, if the subject is singular, the verb should also be singular. Words describing a collective, such as "team," "family," and "group," are singular and should be used with a singular verb. Also, make sure that verbs are written in the correct tense.

6. A cohesive paragraph is composed of a group of related sentences that combine to express a single idea. When you want to express a new idea, indent and begin a new paragraph. Usually a paragraph should begin with a main idea, or topic sentence, and gradually become more detailed and specific. The details of each paragraph should be supported with accurate data.

7. When constructing a document, remember that you are writing for a specific audience. Clearly establish the purpose of your document so you won't confuse the reader.

8. Redundant statements will bore your readers and detract from the effectiveness of your writing. State your point clearly and then move on to new ideas.

9. Briefly summarize the purpose and content of your writing.
10. Keep your purpose in mind. Are you writing to share, collect, or disseminate information? Have you accomplished your intended purpose? After you complete your document, put it aside and reread it a few hours later or, if possible, the next day. Rereading the document later helps you assess your writing objectively.

Writing Memos

When writing a business memo, present information in a clear, logical manner. Before writing, answer at least two of the following questions to establish the information you should include in your memo:

- Why am I writing this memo? Am I writing it to achieve a certain result?
- Who will receive this memo?
- Where will the meeting or event take place?
- What is my plan for accomplishing expected results (methods of action)?

Guidelines for Developing an Agenda Memo:

1. Identify business issues or concerns.
    a. If soliciting for employee opinion, target a specific group and distribute a one-page questionnaire.

      b. Ask that people planning to attend the meeting contribute to agenda items.

      c. Choose topics you think should be discussed.

2. Set a realistic timeframe.

      a. There is no "correct" timeframe for a meeting. However, when meetings run too long, members become bored and restless.

      b. Estimate the amount of time necessary to discuss a specific issue. If you adhere to the time allotted for each agenda item and manage time wisely, many issues can be discussed within an hour.

      c. Clearly state the purpose of the meeting.

      d. If you can conclude the meeting before expected, participants will consider you their hero!

3. Address agenda issues.

      a. Find and communicate with a person who is knowledgeable about the issue you plan to address.

      b. Invite guest speakers to address specific issues. (Guests do not have to stay for the entire meeting.)

4. Distribute the agenda memo seven to ten days prior to the meeting. This should give most

members a chance to work the meeting into their schedules.
5. Use the Premeeting Agenda Memo on the next page for format and content.

SAMPLE PREMEETING AGENDA MEMO

Date: _____

To: (List the people who will attend the meeting and, if necessary, include a list of their departments.)

From: (Your name and department)

Subject: **Meeting concerning**_____

Time _____

Date _____

Place _____

Equipment Needed:_____

Expected Results: _____
                (i.e., purpose of the meeting)

Agenda Items

    Topics, speakers, and time.

    Topics for our next meeting:

Thoughts for Processing an Agenda

1. Use a three-hole punch so the agenda pages can be stored easily in binders.
2. Encourage note-taking on the agenda page.
3. Begin each meeting with a discussion of follow-up from the last meeting.
4. Only so much information can be collected, shared, and disseminated in a meeting. Don't try to cram too much information into a given meeting time.
5. Create a relaxed atmosphere but, at the same time, maintain control and direction over the group and the meeting.
6. Check the sample meeting agenda on the following pages for some ideas on format and what content to include in your agendas.

The Meeting

During the meeting, acknowledge and discuss business needs with the group. Listen with an open mind to everything said; don't ignore input you might not want to hear. Let group members express their opinions without rebuttal. Also remember to:

- Identify the business issues to be addressed. Target a specific group or attending members to discover their concerns about the issues.
- Make sure to inform appropriate decision-makers of the meeting.

- Brainstorm within the group to exchange information and ideas about issues and, if possible, resolve them. Ask the group to summarize the issues and devise an action plan.
- Set up guidelines to help you and the group assess the quality and effectiveness of the action plan.
- While planning the next meeting, list follow-up actions on the agenda.
- As part of your follow-up, distribute notes from the meeting within forty-eight hours of its conclusion.

Don't discard the agenda after a meeting; keep it on file as a record and historical perspective for future meetings and presentations.

The agenda is crucial to the success of a meeting because it provides focus as well as a guideline for the flow of information. The sample agenda on the following pages is a guide to help you organize your meetings. Note that it follows the same concepts of presentation design introduced earlier. Also note that there is an additional five minutes of time between agenda items. No meeting will ever be so restricted as to adhere to a minute-by-minute schedule. Give leeway to the time schedule with these additional five minute periods.

MEETING AGENDA SAMPLE
(Title of Meeting)

People in attendance:_____

Date: _____

Expected Results: (What is to be accomplished?) _____

Meeting Begins_____*1:10*_____

1. Topic: Decision(s):_____

   Time to discuss:

   (10 mins 1:15—1:25 p.m.)   Action(s) to be taken: __

   Discussion led by:

                              Timeframe to
                              accomplish:_____

2. Topic: Decision(s):_____

   Time to discuss:

   (15 mins 1:30—1:45 p.m.)   Action(s) to be taken: __

   Discussion led by:

                              Timeframe to
                              accomplish:_____

3. Topic: Decision(s):_____

   Time to discuss: _____

   (40 mins 1:50—2:30 p.m.) Action(s) to be taken: __

   Discussion led by: _____

                             Timeframe to
                             accomplish:_____

                             _____

Summary and Closing

(10 mins)

Conclude approximately
2:45 p.m.

CHAPTER 7

FEEDBACK

"Performance evaluation is essential—more than ever, in fact. It is a tool for directing attention, and attention today must be directed to new targets."

(Peters, 1987, p. 495)

    As a presenter, you have the option of collecting information from your audience concerning your presentation and how well you met their needs. This information provides valuable feedback on your presentation skills and helps you determine what follow-up information is necessary to supplement your presentation. Following is an easy-to-use survey designed to focus on the audience's needs.

AUDIENCE SURVEY

1. Were you satisfied with the content covered in today's presentation?

   Not very satisfied   Satisfied   Very satisfied
   _____
         1   2   3   4   5   6   7

   Comments
   _____
   _____

2. Were you satisfied with the specific details presented?

   Not very satisfied   Satisfied   Very satisfied
   _____
         1   2   3   4   5   6   7

   Comments
   _____
   _____

3. Were you satisfied with the length of the presentation?

Not very satisfied			Satisfied		Very satisfied	
1	2	3	4	5	6	7

Comments
_____
_____

4. Were you satisfied with the visuals/handouts?

Not very satisfied			Satisfied		Very satisfied	
1	2	3	4	5	6	7

Comments
_____
_____

5. Were you satisfied with the style of presentation?

　　　Not very satisfied　　　Satisfied　　　Very satisfied

　　　1　　2　　3　　4　　5　　6　　7

Comments
_____
_____

6. Were you satisfied with the speaker's methods of presenting?

　　　Not very satisfied　　　Satisfied　　　Very satisfied

　　　1　　2　　3　　4　　5　　6　　7

Comments
_____
_____

7. Were you satisfied with follow-up materials?

Not very satisfied	Satisfied	Very satisfied

1   2   3   4   5   6   7

Comments
_____
_____

General Comments
_____
_____
_____
_____

     This survey takes only a few moments to complete, yet it offers you valuable insights for your next presentation.

Completing an Action Plan

An action plan is your honest evaluation of your last presentation; it acts as a guide for improving your presentation skills. Your action plan should be both supportive and corrective. Challenge yourself with this self-assessment process: Try to acknowledge what was or was not appropriate for the presentation. Always look at each presentation as a learning experience.

To assess your next presentation, ask yourself these questions:

1. Why did I present this information?

   _____
   _____
   _____

2. Did my presentation start with an overview, move to analysis, and end with a summary?

   _____
   _____
   _____

3. Did my presentation meet the needs of the audience?

   _____
   _____
   _____

4. What would I change in the presentation to better suit my presentment skills?

_____
_____
_____

5. What visual aids did I use to support my presentation (video, audio, graphics)?

_____
_____
_____

6. Were the visual aids successful? Why or why not?

_____
_____
_____

7. Was I aware of my body skills (voice, hands, inflection, eye contact)?

_____
_____
_____

8. What changes should I make concerning my body skills?
   _____
   _____
   _____

9. How did I draw the audience into my presentation?
   _____
   _____
   _____

10. What is my overall rating of the presentation? Why?
    Excellent _____   Satisfactory _____   Poor _____

11. Follow-up actions:
    A. What did I do well that I want to continue?
       _____
       _____

    B. What do I want to correct?
       _____
       _____

Feedback

12. Reflect on your presentation ability, the audience's ability to comprehend, the environment (room temperature, lighting, room setup, equipment). Did you meet your audience's needs? Did you accomplish what you wanted?

    _____
    _____
    _____

13. General Comments:

    _____
    _____
    _____

                        Date _____

IN CLOSING

"Education—or even better, learning—must now be defined as a lifelong process. The primary learning during youth will be the skills of inquiry and the learning after schooling will be focused on acquiring the knowledge, skills, understanding, attitude, and values required for living adequately in a rapidly changing world.

(Knowles, 1975, p. 16)

Now that you have examined these presentation techniques closely, how might you best use them? To get started, choose the techniques that will benefit you most and seem to address your style and problems most clearly. Don't try to incorporate every idea. You are now aware of the variety of components available to help you create and deliver an effective presentation. This book will serve as a resource as you develop a confident and effective presentation style. Remember that a skillful presenter practices, accepts and applies feedback, and makes fun a part of this process.

Practice — Become conscious of your presentation style by giving presentations and reviewing them. Stand in front of a mirror and notice the facial expressions you use when you present. Make your presentation to anyone who will listen, including the family pet. When you have no audience to practice on, go over the steps of your presentation mentally, as though you were giving it. Familiarize yourself with your presentation, but do not memorize it. Adaptability—of your material and your style—is essential to a flexible relationship with your audience.

Feedback — Collect as much information as you can from your audience and yourself. If possible, videotape your presentation so you can examine your presentation style. Never criticize yourself excessively or unconstructively. Ask for feedback from a business associate or your audience. In reviewing for presentation feedback, look for trends of supportive and corrective feedback. Be careful not to overreact to one or two extreme suggestions. And try to incorporate something new each time you present.

In Closing

To help you collect constructive feedback, examine the instruments in Chapter 7. Keep in mind that the point of collecting feedback is not to dwell on what you did, but how you can improve or enhance your future presentations.

Fun — Anxiety is part of living and, given the ways we view and react to the people around us, it will probably always be a part of effective presentation. We all get nervous, but creating a presentation, recreating it for your audience, and then receiving credit for your good work can be fun. Allow yourself to be creative, to take risks, and give yourself the opportunity to express your ideas. A presentation exists only between you and the listener. Enjoy that unique rapport.

Good luck!

Rex P. Gatto, Ph.D.

REFERENCES

Albrecht, K., Zemke, R. (1985). *Service America!* Homewood, Illinois: Dow Jones-Irwin.

Bandler, R., Grinder, J., & (1979). *Frogs into princes.* Real People Press.

Bennis, W., Nanus, B. (1985). *Leaders, the strategy for taking charge.* New York: Harper and Row.

Bradshaw, J., & Nettleton, N. (1983). *Human cerebral asymmetry.* New Jersey: Prentice Hall.

Bryant, G. (1984). *The working women report.* New York: Simon and Schuster.

Carnegie, D. (1926). *Public speaking and influencing men in business.* New York: American Book, Stratford Press.

Champagne, D., & Hogan, C. (1981). *Consultant supervision theory and skill development.* Pittsburgh: Champagne and Hogan.

Deep, S., & Sussman, L. (1988). *The manager's book of lists.* Pittsburgh: SDD Publishers.

Eitzen, D. (1978). *In conflict and order: Understanding society.* Boston: Allyn and Bacon, Inc.

Frankl, V. (1985). *Man's search for meaning.* New York: Simon and Schuster Inc.

Gatto, R. (1985). Learning styles based curriculum: left brain/right brain dominance. Achievement Motivation and Success. Washington C.C.: Educational Leadership Council of America, Inc.

Gatto, R. Training programs should include a participant's understanding of self. Pittsburgh Times-Journal. 29 July 1985: 1s.

Hall, J. (1988). *Model for management, the structure of competence.* The Woodlands, Texas: Woodstead Press.

Karp, H. (1985). *Personal power an unorthodox guide to success.* New York: American Management Association.

Knowles, M. (1973). *The adult learner: A neglected species.* Houston: Gulf Publishing Company.

Knowles, M. (1975). *Self-directed learning.* New York: Cambridge.

Knowles, M., & H. (1972). *Introduction to group dynamics.* New Jersey: Cambridge.

Lawless, D. (1979). *Organizational behavior: The psychology of effective management.* New Jersey: Prentice Hall.

Luft, J. (1984). *Group process.* San Francisco: Mayfield Publishing Co.

May, R. (1989). *The art of counseling.* New York: Gardner Press.

Mussen, P., Conger, J., Kogan, J., & Geiwitz, J. (1979). *Psychological development: a life span approach.* New York: Harper and Row Publishers.

Peters, T. & Waterman, R. Jr. (1982). *In search of excellence.* New York: Harper and Row Publishers Inc.

Peters, T. (1987). *Thriving on chaos.* New York: Alfred A. Knopf.

Skinner, B.F. (1976). *About behaviorism.* New York: Vintage.

Springer, S., & Deusch, G. (1981). *Left brain, right brain.* San Francisco: W. H. Freeman Co.

Yeomans, W. (1985). *1000 things you never learned in business school.* New York: MacGraw Hill Book Co.

VIDEO

"Be Prepared to Speak" by Kantola. Skill Production, 152, 17th Avenue, San Francisco, California 94121 (415) 752-9897.

INVENTORIES

Brewer, J. Communication style. Organization Design and Development Inc. (215) 279-2002.

Gatto, R. Listening styles inventory. GTA Press (412) 344-2277.

Gatto, R. Visual vs. verbal communication inventory. GTA Press (412) 344-2277.

Glaser, R. Interpersonal influence inventory. Organization Development and Design (212) 279-2002.

BOOKS AND ARTICLES BY REX P. GATTO

"Change—Pittsburgh's downpayment toward the 21st century." (1986-87). Unmistakably Pittsburgh.

Dealing with stress in the workplace: how you handle what happens. (1990). Pittsburgh: GTA Publication.

"Evaluation should not be tied to profit margin." (1985). Pittsburgh Business Times-Journal. 16 Dec. : 13s, 16s.

"Learning styles based curriculum: left brain/right brain dominance." (1984).Achievement Motivation and Success. 8th Annual National Conference of the Educational Leadership Council of America. 11 May: 9-14.

"Training programs should include a participant's understanding of self." (1985). Pittsburgh Business Times-Journal 29 July: 1s, 16s.

What is education? (1988). Dynamic Business, November.

Whole brain concept: its impact on participant learning—understanding yourself to better understand others. (1985). Pittsburgh: GTA Publications.